NOTES FROM THE UNDERGROUND

D0735992

NOTES FROM THE UNDERGROUND

The Spiritual Journal of a Secular Priest

DONALD COZZENS

ORBIS BOOKS

Maryknoll, New York 10545

Founded in 1970, Orbis Books endeavors to publish works that enlighten the mind, nourish the spirit, and challenge the conscience. The publishing arm of the Maryknoll Fathers and Brothers, Orbis seeks to explore the global dimensions of the Christian faith and mission, to invite dialogue with diverse cultures and religious traditions, and to serve the cause of reconciliation and peace. The books published reflect the views of their authors and do not represent the official position of the Maryknoll Society. To learn more about Maryknoll and Orbis Books, please visit our website at http://www.maryknollsociety.org.

Library of Congress Cataloging-in-Publication Data

Cozzens, Donald B.
    Notes from the underground : the spiritual journal of a secular priest / Donald Cozzens.
    pages cm
    ISBN 978-1-62698-006-8 (cloth)
    ISBN 978-1-62698-121-8 (pbk)
    1. Church renewal—Catholic Church.   2. Catholic Church—Doctrines.   3. Catholic Church—History—20th century.
4. Catholic Church—History—21st century.   5. Christianity and culture.   I. Title.
BX1746.C675 2013
282.09'051—dc23
                                                          2012039980

HOPE

PREFACE TO THE PAPERBACK EDITION

As DUSK GAVE WAY TO DARKNESS in St. Peter Square on March 13, 2013, a shooting star of hope lit up the hearts and minds of countless discouraged and dispirited Catholics longing for a healthier, holier, and more humble church. Holding their collective breaths, the faithful watched an obscure Argentinean prelate step out of the shadows into the spotlight of the world's stage.

Wearing a simple white cassock, Jorge Mario Bergoglio, now Pope Francis, did what none of his predecessors had ever done—he bowed to the mass of cheering faithful below the balcony of St. Peter's Basilica. In this exquisite gesture of humility, he bowed not only to the thousands gathered in St. Peter's Square, he bowed to the world. And the Catholic world collectively caught its breath.

To the waving throng below, Francis asked—the voice gentle but steady—that before he blessed them they might prayer *over* him, that they might bless him. "And now I would like to give the blessing, but first—first I ask a favor of you: before the Bishop blesses his people, I ask you to pray to the Lord that he will bless me: the prayer of the people asking the blessing for their Bishop. Let us make, in silence, this prayer: your prayer *over* me." Along with millions of others glued to television screens, I asked myself what this humble gesture and this disarming request for a prayer-blessing might mean. And what did it signal?

In an instant, the silent prayer drew the pope, the thousands in the square, and the millions watching into a virtual holy communion. How could anyone, standing on the balcony of St. Peter's Basilica, stage-center of Catholicism's triumphalism and baroque grandeur, radiate such humility and authenticity? Effortlessly, his spontaneous request for a blessing turned the beam of the world's spotlight from himself to the people below, from the shepherd onto the flock. *Pray over me. Bless me.* I am standing here, he seemed to say, *for* you, for you the People of God. I'm here to give you hope, to walk with you into the new life promised by Jesus Christ.

ALSO IN MARCH 2013, on an infinitely minor scale of significance, Orbis Books published this journal. With a nod to Dostoyevsky, the title captured my experience of Church and priesthood—I was living, as I report here, in a virtual underground. Now, more than a year later, I am on my way up from the underground. I am still adjusting to the light and fresh air of Pope Francis' papacy, but with each breath my lungs fill with hope and the promise of healing for our wounded Church and world. Already there are signs that Francis is mending the tattered credibility and moral authority of the Church's leadership.

And to the surprise of many, Francis' humility and authenticity—not to mention his candor and simplicity—caught the attention of the world's media masters. His social capital, his moral credibility as the world's spiritual leader, went off the charts. *Time Magazine*'s named Francis their Person of the Year for 2013, and soon after he made the covers of the *New Yorker* and *Rolling Stone*. Skeptical secularists were writing featured journal articles and glowing op-ed pieces. Journalists and Vatican watchers reported that since Bergoglio's election, there were signs, tentative to be sure, that simplicity was trumping triumphal display and humility was softening the regal accretions of the Vatican court.

With the exception of nervous traditionalists, Pope Francis' emphasis on mercy and compassion has inspired hope where but a short time ago there was hardening discouragement. People now speak of a "Francis Factor," reporting they are less cynical about the institutional church and more likely to practice their faith. The new pope speaks and acts like a pastor—a pastor who understands the moral confusion and social estrangement that make our human journey so difficult and challenging. Catholics can hardly believe what they read: "The Eucharist . . . is not a prize for the perfect," Francis writes, "but a powerful medicine and nourishment for the weak. . . . Frequently, we act as arbiters of grace rather than its facilitators. But the Church is not a tollhouse; it is the house of the Father, where there is a place for everyone, with all their problems."*

We Catholics now have a pope whose joy, authenticity, and humility inspire and challenge us at the same time. Like the first hints of spring, currents of hope are reviving a weary people. We lift our heads as Francis calls us to Gospel joy and to genuine concern for the poor. There is energy in the air as Francis urges bishops and priests to risk the comforts of the rectory for the insecurity of the streets.

Years in the underground can make one wary. Will Francis really be able to navigate the stormy waters rocking the Church's boat? Knotty, intertwined, and historically embedded issues—calcified clericalism and patriarchy, the role of women in Church life, financial scandals, clergy abuse of minors and the absence of bishops' accountability among others—will continue to challenge this pope. So some tell me to temper my hope, to wait and see. Perhaps I should heed this advice. But Francis has inspired in me a hope that is stronger than my doubts. I suspect the underground darkness will con-

---

* Pope Francis, *The Joy of the Gospel*, 47.

tinue to give way to the light and fire ignited by this wise and humble shepherd from Argentina.

In the meantime, dear reader, may my years in the underground and my wrestling with the issues revealed in this spiritual journal give you comfort and company on your own journey of faith.

FAITH

SOME YEARS AGO, CERTAINLY BY the early 1980s, I came to feel, and soon to think, that I belonged to an underground church. The realization of this state of affairs, this state of my religious and spiritual awareness, dampened my spirit and tested my confidence in a number of relationships with friends, colleagues, and students. It left me disoriented, slightly out of place—as if traveling alone in a foreign land—and much of the time unsure of my identity as a priest. This was rather strange since priesthood, I had long sensed, was my down deep truth, my way of following Christ and the Gospel. Still, I continued to be uncomfortable in the presence of clergy and laity who easily conformed without any apparent distress or discomfort to every directive and pronouncement that came down from on high. It helped to think of myself as a pilgrim in a pilgrim church, even though much of the time I felt out of step. There was no denying it. I was out of step with Vatican policies and directives that ignored or discounted the lived experiences of ordinary women and men, single, married, and divorced. I was out of step with a Vatican that insisted gay and lesbian Catholics were "disordered" and had no right to fall in love. And I was out of step with hierarchs that shrugged off the voices—muted voices though they were—of discouraged and dispirited priests.

Yet I remained in step with the core of the Catholic faith—at least I hoped that was true. My quest for a right and authentic relationship with the divine mystery we call God, I had to trust, was sincere. I willingly surrendered to the life-giving Gospel of Jesus the Christ. I caught the paradox of the Paschal Mystery—that death to my ego led to liberating and joyful life in the presence of God. There were times, frequent times, when I experienced the presence of the Spirit holding me in communion with others, with creation itself. All this, I understood, was intimately linked to my membership in the church. My struggle, I discovered, was to be "my own man" and a man of the church. Even as I write it, I don't like the sound of "my own man." I don't mean I want to be some kind of lone ranger, some kind of radical individualist or libertarian marching to his own arrogant drumbeat. What I do mean is that I wanted to be an adult man. I wanted to be a churchman, if you will, who understands, if ever imperfectly, that we become adults—our own person—when we experience the blessed communion we discover in the community we call church. In this divine milieu we are encouraged to think freely and creatively both as individuals and as a community, to draw without fear on the creative energy of our imagination, and to celebrate the extraordinary, global connectedness embedded in God's creation.

This underground church, I've come to see, consists of men and women whose first desire is to be simply adult—a church not of children or adolescents hesitant to think and reflect on the lessons of human experience and their efforts to live the Gospel, but rather a pilgrim people who believe the Holy Spirit is loose in the world and whose rumors of wisdom might be found in any of God's people as well as in their ordained leaders.

I'm hardly alone in the underground church. I take comfort in that. And it's my comrades in faith as much as the Spirit that gives me hope. These include friends from different walks of life—teachers and theologians, contemplative nuns and priests—who have sat at table with me deep into the evening discussing Jesus' message and the mysteries of grace in our conflicted church and world. Like Cleopas and his companion at the Emmaus supper, my heart was often enough burning with what I dare to call a moment of transcendence, a taste of the reality Jesus called the Reign of God. This table fellowship, what Walter Brueggemann has described as "serious conversation leading to blessed communion," has held me firm in the fold of the church.

But I fear the above-ground church, the church of the hierarchs, is wary of serious conversation by those outside the circle of sacred purple. More often than not, church authorities appear far more interested in pious docility from the laity and lower clergy. "Leave the heavy thinking and theologizing to us," they say indirectly, often in the high-blown language of all-wise parents speaking to adolescent children. When they speak this way, they give themselves away. Believing they alone are the guardians of the church's sacred doctrines, they can't help but dictate what is to be believed and practiced. Now a well-educated Catholic laity is saying in effect, "We don't take dictation." But many, we might say most, of the hierarchy continue to see their role solely as teachers and governors—and not also as listeners and learners.

So, I'm likely to live out my years in the underground, holding fast to the hope of a renewed and reformed church envisioned by Pope John XXIII, a church open to the currents of grace flowing through cathedrals and marketplaces, through chanceries and ghettos, through ordinary women and men, through the multitudes of people of good will. Perhaps in the underground, I'm closer to the spirit of Pope John, to Teilhard de Chardin and Yves Congar, to Thomas Merton and Dorothy Day (described once as a Mother Teresa with a past). May these servants of the church keep me in step with the truth of the Gospel.

The image of an underground, reminiscent of the French underground during World War II and the Catholics who practiced their faith in secret and at their own peril during the years of Communist control in Central and Eastern Europe, is, I admit, a tricky conceit. When the Soviet machine repressed Christianity in East Germany, Poland, and the Baltic States, there was, indeed, an underground church where the faithful stood in real danger of arrest, interrogation, and much worse. Still, the image of an underground seems strangely appropriate even in this postconciliar period in which the teaching church proclaims—albeit in a shaky, halting voice— that the church is now and always will be in need of renewal and reform.

Especially with the so-called pelvic issues, it's deemed prudent to speak cautiously about reform and renewal. More often by inference than edict, the message is passed to priests, for example, that optional celibacy for diocesan priests is not to be the subject of conversation, especially not in the media. Nor are clergy and theologians to speak or write about the laity's nonreception of the Vatican teaching prohibiting artificial forms of birth control or the role of women in the church. A pastor who believes gay and lesbian parishioners are not disordered in their sexual orientation is likely to think twice about saying so from the pulpit or in his parish bulletin. These are not matters of divine revelation. But in our polarized church, they might as well be. Many traditional Catholics appear to believe such issues are indeed within the church's dogmatic pale and therefore closed to investigation, study, and debate. And these same Catholics have a real, if subtle, inquisition to shore up their mission for Catholic uniformity rather than for church unity. I know the Congregation for the Doctrine of the Faith has an important responsibility for the integrity and unity of the Catholic communion. I'm thinking here more of self-appointed guardians of orthodoxy who have taken on the role of inquisitors who can anonymously report individuals they suspect of doctrinal deviancy to the Vatican.

As the vision and reforms of the Second Vatican Council continue to be rolled back, a large segment of the Catholic community energized by the Council's constitutions, decrees, and declarations sense they are now out of step with the Roman authorities of their church. It is this atmosphere of suspicion and accusation that has dispirited countless Catholics in today's church. I confess here that I am one of them. And so what this journal comes down to is simply notes from the underground, my determined attempts to hold fast to the hope, peace, and joy of the Gospel.

————•◆•————

IT HAD TO BE MY parents and grandparents and the nuns and priests of my youth who made belief come naturally to me. Their world of faith became my world of faith. And securely embedded in this community I discovered early on a sense of the sacred. It was pure gift. I didn't have words for it then as a ten-year-old altar server, but I sensed, even knew, that there was a hidden dimension to life, a mysterious yet vital reality just under the surface of everyday living. How this sense of the sacred was linked to my catechism's canon of church teachings, I had only the vaguest idea. But my early sense of awe at the mystery dimension of life went beyond the propositional declarations of belief I was learning to memorize and take to heart.

Was this inner glow, this inner sense of the divine presence, a delusion? Was my innocent sense of the reality of mystery but a fiction? Perhaps. But my young spirit somehow had been touched by the burning coals of grace—and from then on I would hold to the belief that the Spirit crouched in the everyday corners of my life. The sacred was indeed present. In the bread and wine of Eucharist, of course. In the sacramental life of the church, of course. But as a young man I came to see that the divine was hidden in the most pedestrian details of ordinary life.

Could this be true? Did the divine rest hidden in the ordinary comings and goings of the secular city, in the routine of commuters and stay-at-home parents, in the breezy conversations of young professionals at their end-of-the-day watering holes?

THE SEPTEMBER AFTER GRADUATING from high school, I began studying for the priesthood with the understanding that faith meant intellectual assent—*obsequience*—to the official teachings of the Roman Catholic Church. If I believed what the church lifted up as essential doctrine, then I was a man of faith. Belief was but another name for faith. And conversely, faith was but another name for belief. The cheery mantra, "Keep the faith," meant simply to hold fast to the dogmas and doctrines and disciplines of the Catholic Church. I never gave it a second thought.

IN THE MONTHS BEFORE I was ordained a priest, my paternal grandfather, Joseph Patrick Cozzens, lay dying in St. Alexis Hospital in Cleveland. I visited him in the black suit, white shirt, and black tie of a seminarian. I remember wishing I could anoint him—celebrate with him the Sacrament of the Sick. Both he and my grandmother, Ella Brennan Cozzens, were proud beyond words that their grandson would soon be ordained. As I sat next to his bed, he said with a seriousness I'll never forget, "Don, be a good priest." The words were like a stamp on my soul. "Be a good priest." My grandfather knew a good number of priests and was a founding lay trustee of St. Timothy's, a daughter parish of Holy Name Church where my great-great-grandparents settled in the early 1840s. It was only years later that I came to suspect he knew priests well enough to have seen their dark side, their strained efforts to deal with the loneliness of celibacy, the tendency to avarice and drink that left their mark on a good number of them.

What did his "Be a good priest" mean? Did he mean that he wanted me to preach the Gospel, tend to the pastoral needs of my parishioners, be available as their spiritual guide? Or did my grandfather mean that he feared I might succumb to the temptations that weighed heavy on the priests he knew—sliding into the good life, comfortable rectory living, good food and drink, and the seductive comforts of the country club set? Or worse, the comforts of a mistress? The idea that priests could abuse young boys was, I'm sure, inconceivable to him as it was to me and most Catholics in the 1960s, save, of course, the victims of priest pederasts. Now, approaching fifty years as a priest, I believe I know what my grandfather meant. He wanted me to be a man of faith and prayer, a man of the church, and my own man. Over the years I've grown in respect for my grandfather's understanding of the dangers inherent in the priesthood—its agonies and ecstasies. Joseph Patrick Cozzens knew what his grandson was getting into.

Years after my grandfather's death, through a gradual maturation of my interior life, I did give a second thought to what "Keep the faith" meant. It went beyond and deeper than dogmas, doctrines, and disciplines. What if faith and belief had, in fact, their own religious territory and boundaries? What if they were distinct enough that a Christian who doubted or struggled to accept certain church doctrines might still be a person

of faith? Could it be that a Christian who embraced all
the official teachings of the church might, in the end, be
faithless?

Faithful Doubters

SATURDAY MORNINGS ARE SPECIAL FOR ME—sacred even.
For more than two decades now I meet with a dozen or
so friends for coffee and conversation. I've dubbed us
"the coffee house theologians." Often as we discuss various issues relating to religion and spirituality, to church
and society, I remember Brueggemann's insight: "What
we are about is serious conversation leading to blessed
communion." What's kept the coffee house theologians
gathering each Saturday these many years is the grace
of serious conversation that regularly leads to a certain
level of blessed communion. We are mostly "Vatican
II Catholics" who hope for a more inclusive church, a
more humble church, a church that is willing to judge
itself by the same core truths and values with which it
judges secular society. In other words, we dare to hold
ourselves and our prelates to the noble notion that the
church, as a pilgrim church, will always be a wounded
church in need of healing reform.

In recent years we've been joined by a witty curmud-
geon named Joseph Michael Foley, a Harvard trained
neurologist with an elephant's memory and a lion's

faith. He went to daily Mass until his legs slowed him down. (He died peacefully at the age of 96 in July 2012.) Joe Foley was a life-long, loyal Catholic to his core. If his legs betrayed him, his keen intellect certainly didn't. One Saturday morning, the light in his blue eyes dimmed and his features took on the gravitas of ultimate concern. "I'm afraid," he said in a whisper reminiscent of the confessional, "I'm a heretic." He held our attention for a moment before going on. Then in a resigned but firm voice, Dr. Foley confessed, "I can't accept the dogma of the Assumption. I just can't believe it." What followed was a display of his world-class intellect. He quoted from memory, to no one's surprise, the salient sentence from Pope Pius XII's 1950 apostolic constitution. "We pronounce, declare, and define it to be a divinely revealed dogma: that the Immaculate Mother of God, the ever Virgin Mary, having completed the course of her earthly life, was assumed body and soul into heavenly glory."[1] Where did she go? he wondered. And how did she get there? Did Mary require nourishment? Joe Foley was not only a Catholic to his core, he was a scientist to his core.

"It's a mystery, Joe," I said. The "M" word made him wince. No explanation or theological interpretation of the meaning or significance of the Pope's declaration seemed to help. It was clear to this renowned scientist that appeals to mystical or metaphysical or metaphorical interpretations of the dogma wouldn't satisfy his need to understand the "how" of the Assumption. For Joseph Foley, if there was a tear in his assembled coat of Christian beliefs, there was a dent in his armor of faith.

THE DEPOSIT OF FAITH, the "Catholic Ark of the Covenant," seems to be more a "Deposit of Beliefs." Just a few centuries after Jesus' death and resurrection, we fashioned our core beliefs into creedal statements that have stood the test of time, giving the followers of Christ an embracing identity and a sure foundation for their unity in diversity. Both the Nicene and Apostles' Creeds were forged in the fire of doctrinal disputes that led to banishments, violent conflict, and tragic schisms. Now, centuries old, the two creeds remain central to our faith in Jesus Christ. But propositional statements of belief are not equivalent to biblical faith. I try to remember this when parents of my university students stop by my office when visiting the campus. From time to time, the conversation goes something like this. "Father, would you pray for my daughter. She's lost her faith. She doesn't go to Mass anymore." Implicit in this request is the concerned parent's awareness of the church's teaching that it's a mortal sin to miss Sunday Mass. If her daughter is regularly missing Mass, the parent fears she is rejecting this teaching, And worse, rejecting her faith. Sometimes the student in question, the not-at-Mass-every-Sunday delinquent, spends every Friday evening with other students handing out sandwiches and coffee to homeless men and women of our city. She's the kind of young Catholic who uses her spring break for an immersion service trip to a Central American country. She may no longer believe it is a mortal sin to miss Mass on Sunday, and she may indeed be struggling with a crisis of belief, but not for a moment do I believe she has lost her faith.

THIS PAST WEEK A GRADUATE student from a nearby university came to see me. I'll call her Sarah. Bright, attractive, and articulate, she is struggling to maintain her integrity in the face of an authentic crisis of faith. But in her case, the crisis is double-barreled. She assures me she believes in God, but beyond that there is nothing but doubt when it comes to Christ, the church, and the sacraments. She has been going to Mass of late, but at least once she had to abruptly leave the church overwhelmed with anxiety and confusion. And her anxiety is snowballing. Engaged to a Catholic man, the prospect of a church wedding in her present state of doubt has plunged her into a spiraling state of angst and confusion. Sarah's mother, it turns out, is an ultra-conservative Catholic, and their relationship, understandably, is strained. Being married "outside the church," she is certain, would crush her parents and grandmother, and she believes, her fiancé's parents and grandparents as well.

Moreover, her friends think of her as an agnostic, and they certainly would see a church wedding as hypocritical. But Sarah's most urgent crisis, she understands, is existential. It's about her own integrity, her own authenticity. Filled with doubt, not sure she can even pray, how can she ever marry in the church? Sarah continues her struggle to hear the voice of her conscience. In the midst of her doubt, her goodness shines through.

> The line between belief and unbelief
> runs through the middle of each one of us—
> including myself, a bishop of the church.

> — Cardinal Carlo Martini

I PRAY FOR JOE FOLEY, for students who don't go to Mass, for Sarah, and for myself—priest, professor of theology— and one who himself doubts. And I pray for all who doubt, for all who struggle to be faithful to the mystery we call God. I pray for those who doubt various dogmas and doctrines of their religion and still courageously trust in the hidden presence of God, who cling to membership in their church when they see corruption of all sorts in their ordained leaders. I pray, too, for all who have been wounded in truly horrendous ways by ecclesiastical power holders and clerical pedophiles. If there is such a thing as righteous anger, then there must be such a thing as righteous doubt. And I pray for those who have no doubts, for those who have repressed their doubts under a blanket of simple, nonthinking obedience to church pronouncements and directives of every stripe.

SO THE DISTINCTION I'VE NOTED between faith and belief continues to intrigue me, especially when I look at what Jesus said about faith. In the second chapter of Mark, Jesus is teaching in Capernaum, perhaps in Peter's house, and the place is packed to overflowing. A paralyzed man, carried along on a mat or some kind of stretcher by his friends, approaches the house hoping to see the carpenter from Nazareth turned healer. The man who couldn't walk has some creative friends who find a way to make an opening in the roof of the house and let him down through the ceiling with a soft landing right in front of Jesus. And Mark reports that "When Jesus saw their *faith*, he said to the paralytic, 'Son, your sins are forgiven . . .' And then Jesus said to the man, 'I say to you, stand up, take your mat and go to your home.'"

Jesus saw *their faith*. . . . What was the nature of this faith that Jesus saw in the eyes of the paralyzed man and his friends? They certainly weren't enrolled in the Rite of Christian Initiation of Adults nor did they have the benefit of hours of "instructions" from the pastor in the parish rectory. What did Jesus see? He saw there fundamental goodness, their instinctive trust that he was a man of God with a message from God. And he saw their hope that one of them might be able to walk again.

What did Jesus see? Jesus saw their faith—a faith absent of doctrinal content in the sense of dogmas and creedal formulas. What did Jesus see? He saw their trust in the ultimate goodness of God, a glimpse of which they saw in the healer from Nazareth.

And in the seventh chapter of Luke's Gospel, a woman known as a sinner crashes a dinner party for Jesus thrown by a prosperous Pharisee. "She stood behind him at his feet, weeping, and began to bathe his feet with her tears and to dry them with her hair. Then she continued kissing his feet and anointing them with the ointment." It caused quite a stir. And to everyone's surprise, Jesus said to the woman, "Your *faith* has saved you; go in peace." Now this woman, like the paralytic, never enrolled in the RCIA, never attended the Parish School of Religion, never took "instructions" in the faith. For this woman with the dicey reputation and for the paralytic and his friends, faith it appears meant a decision of the heart to trust that Jesus was a man of God, perhaps even the Messiah, the Chosen One. Then and now, trust is the existential core of faith—a steadfast conviction held without proofs of any kind that the mystery we call God is indeed good, that creation itself is holy, that we are called to live in right relationships that emerge in history as a *holy communion*.

But from around the third century, faith became more and more indistinguishable from belief—from assenting to theological propositions about God, Jesus, and revealed truths. Dogmas and doctrines, of course, have a hallowed place in the pilgrim's journey of faith. We might imagine them as sacred vessels holding our sacred trust—our faith—that God is love and that though it might seem too good to be true, God loves us unconditionally. And trusting wholeheartedly in this love, we have nothing to fear.

Dogmas and doctrines—alongside efforts to love our neighbor as ourselves and to see Christ in the poor and the least among us—became the distinguishing marks of the Christian. Intellectual assent to these creedal teachings soon trumped existential trust in the living realities to which they pointed. I remind myself of the existential dimension to faith by making a silent one-word substitution when I recite the Nicene Creed at Eucharist.

> I *trust* in one God, the Father almighty . . .
> I *trust* in one Lord Jesus Christ, the only
>   Son of God . . .
> I *trust* in the Holy Spirit, the Lord, the giver
>   of life . . .
> I *trust* in one, holy, catholic and apostolic Church.

FAITH, THEN, IS FUNDAMENTALLY A cry of the heart, a brave act of trust in the hidden God, a ready-to-risk-all conviction that through God's grace we are in relationship with the divine, that we are God's beloved—that we are saved. That's why the paralytic and his friends were described by Jesus as men of faith. That's why the broken woman who washed Jesus' feet with her tears and anointed them with ointment was a woman of faith. That's why Dr. Foley is a man of faith. And maybe doubting Sarah, struggling to protect her integrity while confessing she is unsure of the place Jesus holds in her life, might too be a woman of faith.

> God is greater than religion,
> faith is greater than dogma.

— Rabbi Abraham Heschel

IT'S HOLY WEEK AS I WRITE, and I find these days dangerous as well as sacred. Remembering and entering into the passion of Jesus of Nazareth easily reinforces the common understanding that God Almighty demanded the torture and death of his only begotten son to appease him for the offense he endured because of the sins of humankind. There is a warped logic at play here— only the death of God's divine son can right the scales of justice in the divinity we call God. This isn't the God preached by Jesus, the God who is, when all is said and done, a God of love and mercy.

For many Catholics today, maybe for most, the atonement theory of Jesus' suffering and death is taken to heart as a dogma of the Christian religion—only

the crucifixion of God's son could atone for the sins of
the world, smooth over the wrath of the Almighty, and
open once again the gates of heaven. But we don't suffer
for our sins, we suffer *from* our sins. That's the message Jesus taught when he told the scandalous story of
the prodigal son. We're loved already, saved already, redeemed already—before we can ever merit God's love,
or be saved by Jesus' passion, or be redeemed by our
entering into the Paschal Mystery. If this isn't the conviction of the person of faith, then we have made a sacrament of suffering and violence.

But for many of the pious and not so pious, they
want salvation the old-fashioned way; they want to
earn it. They're convinced that if they but will it hard
enough, they'll achieve it. And don't trouble their good
consciences with the idea of the Pelagian heresy. We
are saved, therefore, not by willful acts of penance and
righteousness so much as by participating in the life and
death and resurrection of Jesus the Christ.

The Jesuit Karl Rahner put it this way:

> We are at the beginning of Holy Week. If we
> want truly to be Christians, this week ought to
> be a time when we share in a special way in the
> passion of Christ. We do this not so much by
> indulging in pious feelings, but by bearing the
> burdens of our life with simple fortitude and

without ostentation. For we share by faith in the
passion of the Lord precisely by realizing that
our life is a participation in his destiny. We find
this difficult, because so often we fail to understand that the bitterness and burden of our own
life do—or should—give us a mysterious share
in the destiny of all human beings.[2]

IF WE SHARE BY FAITH IN the passion of the Lord and
in his destiny, we share by faith in the fullness of his
life—in resurrection life. Here faith and trust give birth
to Easter hope. Our common destiny is new life in God's
spirit. Fear, envy, and violence are not destined, after all,
to win out in the end. So we muster the courage to trust
our ability to survive the bitterness and burdens of life
through a mysterious sharing in Christ's life, which at
the same time is a mysterious sharing in the very destiny of all human beings. Faith, Rahner helps us see, is
not only trusting in the ultimately benign saving love of
God, it is trusting in the ultimate goodness of creation.
Instead of fearing the secular, that is, the world, we can
trust the hidden presence of the creator in all that we encounter. Our sacred traditions and our sacred scriptures
are "entrusted" to us so that we might draw ever closer
to the fullness of light we Christians confess to see in
Christ. Our doctrines and dogmas, therefore, are meant
to support and nurture our fragile trusting, our fragile

efforts to hold firm to the saving paradox of the Paschal Mystery. Dying with Christ, we rise to life transformed.

ALMOST FROM THE BEGINNING, certainly from the time of Constantine, Christian authorities allowed doctrinal orthodoxy to trump faith, understood, I argue, as a courageous leap of trust in the saving mystery we call God. Harvard's Harvey Cox records the grim fate of Priscillian of Avila who was condemned for heresy by a synod of bishops in 385 and by order of the emperor Maximus was beheaded.[3] He was, we are informed, "the first Christian to be executed by his fellow Christians for his religious views. But he was by no means the last." Early on, the Christian story reveals, it wasn't enough to believe Jesus to be the Christ; one had to believe "correctly" that Jesus was the Christ. Arius, for example, a priest of Alexandria, while believing that Jesus was the Son of God and God's agent in the mighty act of creation, did not believe that Jesus was coeternal with God. "There was a time," Arius held, "when Christ was not."

The priest had many if not most of the early bishops on his side, and the dispute that erupted was not only splitting the Christian body but politically threatening to the Emperor Constantine—threatening enough for the Emperor to call the Council of Nicaea in 325 to settle the matter. Arius lost, of course, but the heresy of Arianism lingered on in some form or other for centuries. Arius suffered exile, but the fate of his supporters was more dire. Constantine decreed that "If any treatise composed by Arius be discovered, let it be consigned to the flames . . . and if anyone shall be caught concealing a book by Arius, and does not instantly bring it out and burn it, the penalty shall be death; the criminal shall suffer punishment immediately after conviction."[4] The die was cast stamping heresy as a crime, in this case a capital crime.

THE CHRISTOLOGICAL CONFLICTS OF THE fourth century are worthy of our respect and they certainly shaped the creedal statements that anchor our Christian deposit of beliefs, but I keep thinking of the heretics who were anathematized and excommunicated—and worse—for not believing in Christ correctly. I winced when I read that the number of martyrs put to death by the pagan emperors notorious for their persecution of the early church is exceeded only by the number of heretics put to death by Christian emperors for their incorrect beliefs.[5] Faith, like love, escapes easy measurement. A question like, "How much do you trust in Christ?" leaves one speechless or mouthing something like, "A lot" or "Pretty much" or "Not much at all." But beliefs, unlike faith, are subject to measurement. We are asked, "Do you believe in Christ, in the Trinity . . . in life everlasting?" And we can answer yes or no or remain silent. And we are asked not only if we believe, some of us are asked to swear that we believe. I was one of those asked to swear.

The Oath

IT HAPPENED SHORTLY BEFORE MY ordination to the priesthood in 1965. But my personal little saga must be put in context. More than a half century earlier, Pope Pius X, alerted to a fast-paced, insidious heresy that was infecting not only the lives of ordinary Catholics, but especially the minds of theologians and seminary professors, took drastic action. The heresy to be squelched was "Modernism, the synthesis of all heresies." And the antidote the pope prescribed was the "Oath against Modernism," which was to be taken by seminary professors at the beginning of each academic year and by seminarians approaching ordination to the priesthood among others. Now my seminary study of theology coincided with the four sessions of the Second Vatican Council and the Council clearly had transcended or repudiated many of the asserted doctrinal positions of the oath. *Moses didn't write the Pentateuch, there was a development of doctrine, the church was the people of God. . . .* At that moment it mattered little how much I trusted that Jesus was the Christ, in other words, my faith. What mattered was that the official church could take some measure of my fidelity to Catholic doctrine, even though the Catholic doctrine to which I was asked to swear was in significant conflict with the teachings of the Second Vatican Council.

I confess that I took the oath. My classmates took the oath. God help me . . . I was soon to be ordained to preach the Word of God, to be a bearer of the Word. My credibility and integrity as a priest, I knew full well, would be grounded in the truth of the words I spoke, especially words sworn to under oath. What had I done? I remember only one comment from a classmate when I confessed my conflicted feelings and guilt at signing the oath. "Oh," he said, "I would have signed anything to be ordained." The off-hand comment said volumes. Didn't I do the very same thing? I felt compromised. I was indeed. My signing of the oath was, perhaps, a minor corruption. A rationalization? No doubt. But hadn't thousands of seminarians throughout the Catholic world done the very same thing? Another rationalization? And not one of us, to my knowledge, raised our voice in protest. Is there such a thing as a minor corruption? I think now of the poet-theologian Kilian McDonnell who wrote these searing lines, "No grand betrayals/ we lacked the impudent will/ we died of small treasons." Small treasons . . . are there any small treasons?

There were pressures, of course. We were just weeks away from the priesthood. The invitations to our ordinations and first Masses—bearing the same social weight as wedding invitations—had been mailed. Receptions and dinners had been planned. Friends and family had made their travel plans. But I had sworn to something I didn't believe. What did that say of me? What does it say of the thousands of men about to be ordained during the years of the Council who swore to the oath knowing as I did that the official teaching of the church had moved far beyond its contents? What does it do to a person's integrity when he swears to something he doesn't hold? Yes, we died of small treasons.

The Vatican requirement that seminarians take the oath against modernism prior to ordination wasn't dropped until 1967.

THE OATH LED ME TO WONDER how many thousands of men and women the church has tortured and burned at the stake for incorrect beliefs—for heresy, that is—who in the eyes of God were men and women of faith nonetheless. Joan of Arc for one. We burned her as a heretic and later declared her a saint. But how many others? I wrestled with this question as I read Cullen Murphy's book on the Inquisition, *God's Jury: The Inquisition and the Making of the Modern World*. As long as Christendom reigned for approximately one thousand years, heresy was not only considered a sin, it was decreed a crime. And as such, a suspected heretic was not only threatened with excommunication, but with arrest, torture, and death at the stake. This fact alone led me to see why the distinction between faith and belief is significant—and why the strict equation of faith with belief in declared doctrines of the church remains problematic. For how can the church measure trust in the mystery we call God? Or one's faith in Jesus as the Christ, or the Spirit's abiding presence? It asks us to say out loud, "I believe." It asks us to swear, "I believe." It follows that the church really can't identify the truly faithful. And never will she be able to admit to that. For then the church would have to forgo her triumphal proclamations of who is in and who is out, of who is faithful and who is not, of who is in communion and who is excommunicated.

Even dissent from noninfallible church teachings like the prohibition of artificial birth control is regarded by church officials and a minority of lay Catholics as a form of heresy. But the church can hardly excommunicate the vast majority of married Catholics who either practice artificial birth control or who fail to see it as sinful. Surely, the already dramatic drop in the percentage of practicing Catholics—measured here by weekly Mass attendance—would plummet even further. The "true believers" say fine. They say we would be better off with a leaner, more "faithful" Catholic church.

The French priest and writer, Jean Sulivan, goes deeper. He sees religious certitude as a form of self-absorption and self-defense against the anxieties and terrors of life. "Their words are buoys; without them they'd completely collapse. Watch the hands and eyes of those who speak [of their religious certitude]. Learn to recognize the faith that reveals a secret despair."[6] But at the same time, the official church will gladly affirm as truly faithful those who firmly proclaim their belief in her dogmas and teachings. Will we ever know, can we ever know, who stands secure in this holy communion we call the church?

South African theologian Albert Nolan, writing with clarity and courage, has identified the crisis traditional Catholics face in light of the Council's teaching. "Upsetting for some people is the undermining of their long held certainties. The challenge they face may not be that of changing one idea for another but rather that of replacing certainties with uncertainty. As we move into a world where many of the things that we took for granted in the past are now being questioned . . . we can cope only by being truly detached from our own ideas and certainties. Obsession with absolute certainty is yet another form of slavery. It is a way of finding security without having to put all our trust in God."[7] But what if our "ideas and certainties" are the bedrock of our religious security? What if we have identified our beliefs in dogmas and doctrines—instead of our faith, that is trust, in Jesus the Christ—as the very foundation of Christianity? These "what ifs" explain the bitter culture wars dividing Catholics. The wars are bitter because in the minds of traditional Catholics, their salvation and the strength of their church is endangered when long-held certainties are even questioned as being in need of development and updating. But Cardinal Newman was right ... there is a "development of doctrine." In this light, the church is a living organism, ever more open, at least in theory, to the inspiration of the Spirit who remains, to the dismay of many, loose in the world. And the Council's humble affirmation that the church is always in need of reform and renewal is reduced to the humanity—and sinfulness—of its individual members, but not to the hierarchic church or its structure and systems. The church as church (here we might weep), is never wrong!

I fear the culture wars' divide, often bitter and accusatory, bodes ill for the near and not so near future of the church, especially in Europe and the Americas. Certainties, especially the religious kind, resist both dialogue and compromise—especially compromise. For the faithful who cannot tolerate doubt, holding to one's religious certitudes is seen as an act of supreme piety, a submissive bow to divinely communicated sacred truths. When this is the case of our religious leaders, interreligious dialogue open to the truth of another religion is seen as a compromise of the church's integrity, or worse, as rank infidelity. The divide that most threatens the Catholic world, however, is intramural: Vatican I Catholics against Vatican II Catholics, traditionalists against progressives, the Roman Curia against local faith communities.

I wish I could see church leaders, that is, bishops and priests, emerging to bridge this tragic divide and courageous enough to address the theological issues widening the breach. But I don't. The only rays of light for me are our theologians, the faithful in the pews, and our college students. That's not quite true. I also find hope in the national associations of priests in Australia, Austria, Ireland, and the United States among others.

THERE IS A KIND OF CERTITUDE of faith, of course. It's what we mean when we say I'm risking all, as St. Paul did, in following Christ. It's what we mean when we say my religion matters most to me. It's what we mean when we say God is our "ultimate concern." But "certitude of faith" taken literally remains an oxymoron. It's an expression meant to capture the believer's firm conviction that the dogmas and doctrines of his or her religion are true. If it were rational certitude, the kind of certitude supported by rigorous logic, it wouldn't be faith in any religious sense. And it implies that all who didn't believe as the true believers believed were in innocent or culpable denial of the logic and "science" undergirding the dogmatic pillars of their religion. "Certitudes" of faith, I must insist, shouldn't be taken literally. It's a manner of speaking when believers who have so committed themselves to their religious beliefs claim an unequivocal "certitude."

But, if taken literally, the claim to certitude is starkly dangerous. It leaves no room for doubt, and doubt is faith's cousin. Ecumenism is then but a sham, and interfaith efforts at dialogue and reciprocal respect are seen as misguided steps toward relativism. And worse, religious certitude lies at the source of religion's justification of persecution, excommunication, and violence. The primal place of conscience is brushed aside, and dissenters in the ranks and members of other religions take on the identity of the enemy. Pogroms, inquisitions, crusades, and righteous "holy wars" waged in the name of God, the history of Western civilization makes painfully clear, inevitably follow.

It's clear to me that the violence spawned by religion or linked to religion grows up and out of religion's various certainties. Religious certitude finds it impossible to tolerate or respect contrary "certitudes," which invariably are denounced as errors, untruths, and heresies. And worse, worthy of persecution and holy war if necessary. It's a marker of human history—sacred violence in the name of religious certitude. I believe this to be true—but tragic "persecutions and holy wars" are too abstract. They let me off the hook. I need to confront and sit with the sobering, convulsing realities of untold thousands of innocent children, women, and men butchered and burned in the name of God. And in the name of my religion.

THE GALILEO AFFAIR COMES TO MIND. It's the classic case study of religious certitude and the blindness it lowers over the eyes of church hierarchs. Religious certitude by its very nature represses uncertainty, which, in turn, is seen alongside dissent as a threat to religious tradition and authority—especially religious authority. Until Galileo the Christian world was certain that the earth was the center of the universe. Predictably, Galileo's assertion that the earth revolved around the sun was condemned by the church in 1633. By the middle of the eighteenth century, only biblical fundamentalists believed the earth remained at the center of it all. But it wasn't until 1822 that Galileo's writings were removed from the index of forbidden books. And still, more telling, it wasn't until the papacy of John Paul II that the church could bring itself to admit that it had been mistaken in condemning the works of Galileo and his immediate scientific predecessor, Nicolaus Copernicus. In November of 1979, while commemorating the centenary of Albert Einstein's birth in an address to the Pontifical Academy of Sciences, Pope John Paul acknowledged that Galileo suffered unjustly at the hands of the church. He admitted, to the surprise of many holding fast to the papacy's legacy of inerrancy and infallibility, that the church had indeed erred and went on to praise Galileo for his authentic religious spirit and for the integrity of his views relating to science and religion.

And so, we might say, the church has come some distance since we marched the philosopher monk Giordano Bruno to the stake in 1600, the last "heretic" to suffer the death penalty for unorthodox beliefs. One of the errors for which he was condemned was holding to the heliocentric theory of Copernicus and Galileo. If indeed we have come some distance from the Inquisition that threatened Galileo's life and snuffed out Bruno's and countless others, there is still a ways to go. I'm thinking of the church's treatment of theologians the caliber of Yves Congar, Pierre Teilhard de Chardin, John Courtney Murray, Hans Küng, Charles Curran, Elizabeth Johnson, Jacques Du Puis, and Tissa Balasuriya among others. I suspect they take some small comfort from the church's action centuries earlier against a most distinguished member of their guild. In 1277, Archbishop Stephen Tempier of Paris condemned 219 errors discovered in the writings of theologians who were drawing on the works of Aristotle. Among the targeted scholars was the great Thomas Aquinas. It was, historians note, the most solemn condemnation of the Middle Ages. While Aquinas' writings were attacked and his works burned, we see in this Dominican a man of deep and profound faith.

OUR BISHOPS, OF COURSE, and the church as a whole, have a responsibility to safeguard the integrity of our deposit of beliefs. In the past, as we know all too well, allegations of erroneous teaching or heresy were pondered and weighed in secret; the suspected offenders were arrested and regularly tortured and not infrequently sent to the stake. Inquisition led to condemnation, and condemnation led to excommunication and sometimes much worse. But there is another way we might go about safeguarding the integrity of our Catholic beliefs. After allowing those charged with false teaching or heresy to confront their accusers and after weighing carefully their alleged false teachings or writings, we might examine the lives of the accused for signs of Christian virtue and right living, for examples of service, generosity, and clear indications of fidelity to the Gospel. If those accused of false teaching are not abiding in the vine that is Christ, there writings will not prevail—so we read in the fifteenth chapter of John's Gospel. If the accused do abide in Christ and their lives bear witness to their faithful trust in Christ, they remain our brothers and sisters. To ignore the context of their fidelity to Christ and the church is at least uncharitable and likely unjust. Then we should let a panel of bishops and theologians examine their work as respected colleagues. And those under suspicion should be at the table to explain and clarify their writings.

This seems like a healthy and adult way to proceed. The mistakes of the past and present cry out for more mature ways to protect the deposit of beliefs.

WHEN THE CELEBRATED GERMAN moral theologian, Bernhard Häring, was interrogated by the Vatican's Congregation for the Doctrine of the Faith (formerly the Holy Office), he compared the experience to what he had suffered at the hands of the Nazis. "During the Second World War," he reported in a memoir, "I stood before a military court four times. Twice it was a case of life and death. At that time I felt honored because I was accused by enemies of God." But to face interrogation by the church he had served all his life? "I would rather stand once again before a court of war of Hitler."[8]

I don't know if the Redemptorist Bernard Häring ever met the Jesuit Walter Burghardt, two of the twentieth century's most distinguished theologians. Both Häring and Burghardt saw the shadow side of the church and understood Cardinal Newman's conviction that it was often necessary to suffer not only *for* the church, but also *from* the church. I hear echoes of Häring's faith—and pain—in this hymn of critique and praise by Burghardt:

> In the course of half a century, I have seen more Catholic corruption than you have read of. I have tasted it. I have been reasonably corrupt

myself. And yet I joy in this church—this living, pulsing, sinning people of God, love it with
a crucifying passion. Why? For all the Catholic
hate, I experience here a community of love. For
all the institutional idiocy, I find here a tradition
of reason. For all the individual repressions, I
breathe here an air of freedom. For all the fear
of sex, I discover here the redemption of my
body. In an age so inhuman, I touch here the
tears of compassion. In a world so grim and humorless, I share here rich joy and laughter. In the
midst of death I hear an incomparable stress on
life. For all the apparent absence of God, I sense
here the real presence of Christ.[9]

Burghardt's point–counterpoint speaks to me. It
helps me understand why Catholics, even Catholics who
know well the church's history of infidelity to the Gospel
and see its present betrayals of the Gospel, stay with the
church—and more, love the church. Yes, and have faith
in the church. We see corruption in the church, and, if
we are honest, we see it in ourselves. We see hierarchs
clinging to their power to ferret out heresy and we see
the church's shepherds holding us in communion. We see
corporate, self-aggrandizing folly and we see a world-
class intellectual tradition championing both reason and
faith. We see the church obsessing over sexuality and we

see the wisdom of her urgent teaching that "sex makes promises." We see grim and repressed clergy and we see pastors whose eyes reflect the compassion of Jesus and whose humor delights our souls.

> Still I put up with this church until I see a
> better one; and she is forced to put up with me,
> until I myself become better.
>
> —Erasmus

STILL, IN AN EARLIER JOURNAL I wrote that I was struggling to remain a priest. It wasn't a crisis of faith, but it was a crisis of integrity. As one of her ordained ministers, I was by that reality a spokesperson for the church, and I was having serious difficulty, not with the church's core beliefs, but with her corporate, "protect the institution at all costs" response to the clergy sexual abuse scandals. *May God have mercy on us.* We church officials—I was vicar for clergy at the time—behaved like any other institution threatened with scandal, sometimes worse. The deadening denial, the legal bullying, the outright lying, and worst of all, the indifference on some occasions to the young boys and girls who suffered seduction and so much worse were all signs of corruption. We officials of the church slogged on in pious self-righteousness, refusing to turn the light of the Gospel on our rigid systems of control, offering, along the way, timid apologies for "mistakes we may have made."

The number of Catholics who left the church in the wake of the scandals is significant. They didn't leave because they doubted the Incarnation or the Trinity or the church's doctrine of grace. They left, I believe, because the *relational* dimension of their faith had been violated. Most, I suspect, held to their faith in God, but their faith in the church had been shattered. For those who stayed, the majority it seems, their confident faith and trust in God, in God's presence in a wounding institution, held them in communion with their fellow parishioners—in spite of the corruption they saw, with such sadness, in their institutional leaders.

Vaclav Havel, the hero of the "velvet revolution," wrote in an open letter to the leader of the Czech government: "The most dangerous road for society: the path of inner decay for the sake of outward appearances; of deadening life for the sake of increasing uniformity."[10] Can't we see that the most dangerous road for the church is "the path of inner decay for the sake of outward appearances; of deadening life for the sake of increasing uniformity"?

I remain a priest and stay in the church because the church is my spiritual home. It's encoded in my DNA. I stay in the church because of the fundamental goodness of the faithful I've come to know and worship with— that's to say I encounter the mystery of God and the communion of saints in the church. I remain a priest because over the years I've come to believe it is my truth, although the essence of the priesthood remains a mystery to me. It's the way I live out my baptism, my discipleship. I remain a priest because I've found grace and holiness in a secular world that struggles to name its spiritual longing. And I want to remain in "the serious conversation that leads to blessed communion." But I remain slightly off balance, sometimes tipping to the edge of despair. Will the church's leaders ever find the courage and humility for ongoing renewal and reform? Will the church ever prize authentic unity over a comforting, yet deceptive uniformity?

Faith, Hope, and Love

No matter their esteemed truth and dignity, dogmas and doctrines are not what we place our hope in. Our hope is grounded in our faith and confident trust in Jesus Christ and the transforming power of the Spirit. Hope doesn't necessarily follow upon doctrinal decrees and "authentic teaching." But it necessarily follows upon authentic faith. Like faith, hope is relational, personal, and a matter far more of the heart than of the intellect. If faith is a "blind leap," then hope is a "courageous confidence" that God remains with us through the darkest hours and that the Reign of God is stronger than any reign of power and control. Hope takes the Paschal Mystery to heart—in dying to our egos and self-will and self-righteousness, we discover new life, new being in God's spirit. We hope in the possibility of transformation of our hearts and imaginations nurtured by the merciful embrace of grace, of "God's affection" for us. Prodigal sons and daughters, we dare to hope that God is ready to run and meet us as we make our first unsure steps back to our true home. And that a grand party awaits us.

Hope, grounded in the Paschal Mystery, allows us to get the joke—that we are saved in Christ and that no earthly calamity can do us in, in any ultimate sense, for "nothing can separate us from the love of God in Christ Jesus." Hilaire Belloc's familiar lines—"Wherever the Catholic sun doth shine, there's always laughter and good red wine. At least I've always found it so, *Benedicamus Domino*"—captures an expression of Christian hope. We can cast our terrible solemnity aside, as Thomas Merton urges, and join in the "general dance."

There are some terribly serious self-appointed church guardians about these days. They worry about the Catholic identity of our colleges and universities; they wring their hands and purse their lips at any movement away from a rigid conformity to doctrinal definitions or to liturgical rubrics. Dissidents, they are sure, are everywhere. For these Catholics who have long forgotten how to laugh and how to dance, the deposit of faith is an ever changeless deposit of doctrines cut in stone. "Modernists," understood as innovators, are everywhere, threatening the age-old faith of their fathers. They can even be found in the ranks of the priests, and God forbid, in the order of bishops. For these "temple police," there can't be too many oaths of orthodoxy, and dissent of any stripe must be treated as heresy. For Catholics of this cut there is no distinction between faith and beliefs. Nor is the Holy Spirit loose in the world blowing where it will. The Spirit is always and only channeled through the hierarchy of the Roman Catholic Church. Without fail, they take themselves very, very seriously. Their only hope is to be forever alert, forever on guard against the church's enemies—both within and without.

IT'S EASTER SEASON NOW AND I ask myself what hope means to me. Without trust in the resurrection of Jesus, my hope, our hope, is groundless . . . nothing but mere optimism that all will eventually work out all right.

My hope doesn't come easy. The hopeful theology, pastoral vision, and liberating spirit of the Second Vatican Council are steadily being smothered. Ecumenism floats listlessly on a windless sea of ecclesiastical triumphalism, and interfaith initiatives remain equally dead in the water. Vowed religious, educated, thinking, faithful women of the church are investigated and censured for daring to run with the spirit of the Gospel as adult disciples of Christ. Lay women and their extraordinary gifts of intellect, talent, and fidelity are kept at the margins of church life. Bishops who ask embarrassing but necessary questions related to the pastoral well-being of their dioceses—like the ordination of married men, the countereffective discipline of mandatory celibacy for diocesan priests, the restricted role of women in ministry—are forced to resign. And priests . . . we're treated like altar boys. Our pastoral experience and the wisdom of years of up-close caring for and leadership of the people of God are routinely discounted. Bishops hardly ever ask us to share with them what we've come to understand about the virtues, struggles, and needs of the Catholic faithful. We are treated like voiceless vassals whose primary responsibility is to strengthen the credibility and dignity of the hierarchy.

No, my hope doesn't come easy. Researchers find that one out of three Catholics leaves the church. One out of ten Americans is a former Catholic. The bleeding hardly seems to distress the bishops. They don't appear interested in *why* Catholics are leaving. I don't think they really want to know. The sexual abuse and financial scandals are reduced to human weakness by a relatively small band of spiritually weak clergy and fiercely distanced from the church's feudal, clerical, and monarchical structures and systems that abetted the scandals.

But still I hope. And most Catholics hope. For hope, along with love, is woven into the fabric of faith. We hope because faith inspires hope as it inspires love. We hope because we have bet our very lives on the life-giving, liberating energy and power of the Gospel. We hope because of Jesus who was always at home with the least of us commoners. We hope because we see through the arrogance of church leaders who confuse rigid orthodoxy and external uniformity with authentic communion. We hope because of the heroic faith and goodness we see in parishioners, our own and the faithful of other religions, who routinely humble those of us in vestments of distinction. We hope because of the dignity we see in the faces of single mothers, the unemployed and homeless, the victims of racism and sexism, and violence of every stripe. And we hope because of the ordinary goodness we see in our families and friends. The kind of ordinary goodness that mostly passes unnoticed.

But I think about the form hope takes, the shape of hope—its existential character. Here's where I hesitate. For the time being, hope for me is courageous, blessed waiting. I wait for the goodness and beauty of being itself to break through the darkness and suspicion of my fractured church, the emptiness and restlessness of my fractured culture, the greed and violence of my fractured world. That's the face of my hope—courageous, patient, peaceful, dare I say joyous, waiting. The trick, of course, is to wait without letting the present moment slip away. The trick is to live fully, mindfully, joyfully in the here and now. On second thought it's no trick. It's grace—the grace of blessed waiting.

Perhaps I'm standing on thin theological ice to write this, but I sometimes think God shares in our waiting for deliverance, that God actually hopes along with us. We Christians, united in faith, are the Body of Christ in history, literally inspired and sustained by his living presence. In this sense, of course, hope took flesh in the man from Galilee. So no one hopes for justice and peace alone. No one hopes for a renewed and reformed church alone. No one hopes alone for the well-being of family and friends, for the healing of the world itself. I believe this, but don't get me wrong; my hope is regularly shoved aside by the sharp elbow of hopelessness. "Get real," it insists. The neoatheists make their case and I pay attention. I grow uneasy trying to turn away from the violence and suffering we inflict on one another. "Hope," the secularists rant, "is hopelessly naïve; better to trust in the NRA than your ephemeral virtue of hope." But I've tried to stake everything—with notable and numerous lapses—on the reality of faith, hope, and love. And, please God, I will continue to stake everything on faith, hope, and love as long as there are friends with whom I can be "about serious conversation leading to blessed communion."

> Everything I know,
> I know only because I love.
>
> —Leo Tolstoy

NOW THERE HAD TO BE SOME among Jesus' disciples who could read and write. Yet the Gospel writers never mention Jesus saying something like, "Now this is important, write it down." That's because Jesus was speaking to his listeners' hearts more than to their minds. He was preaching neither a curriculum nor a catechism, but a new way of life: it's been called "the Way." He spoke of a kingdom that was within, of trusting in God whom he had the nerve to call abba, of honoring the dignity of every man, woman, and child—even among the Gentiles and pagans. Jesus caught his hearers off guard when he said the last shall be first and the least among them the greatest. Some wanted Jesus to state his teachings succinctly in dogmas. He refused. Others wanted Jesus to declare his commandments or to rank the commandments of the Torah. He answered directly and simply: "Love God and love your neighbor as yourself." It's all there, Jesus insisted.

While he underscored the evil of sin and the need for conversion, his emphasis was locked in on loving God and neighbor over everything else—over prayer, over sacrifice, over temple worship.

If faith, as I propose here, is fundamentally relational and hope can be understood as courageous waiting in solidarity for the healing of our fractured church and world, it should be clear that love takes us beyond our egocentric selves. It springs, as St. Augustine discovered, from our deepest desire, recognized or not, for union with God first ("Our hearts are restless, O Lord, until they rest in thee") and for union with others and even with creation itself. It meets our inherent need for transcendence and meaning and some real level of intimacy.

But of the sacred trio of faith, hope, and love, love is the most problematic. Religious faith, understood as religious beliefs, has led believers, as we have seen, to perverse persecutions, including the bloodletting savagery of "holy wars" on those who believe differently, to inquisitions and executions of their own members, to triumphalisms that contradict the humility of all healthy religions. Hope, of course, can be as shallow as a smile button, a cheery optimism and confidence in what we have come to call the "good life," the naïve trust in capital-driven, technology-generated progress. But the misconceptions, false promises, and betrayals of love, at least in terms of individual human suffering, are mountains compared to the foothill grime and grit of misguided faith and hope. The seamless joining of love and faith (and hope, of course) makes the human experience of love's exhilarating joys and heartbreaking disappointments match the emotional consolations and desolations of religious faith. For the believer, love and faith are two sides of the same coin.

Some days I think I know something about love. Other days I don't know a thing about it. I think love is like humility. As soon as I believe I'm humble, I'm not. As soon as I congratulate myself for loving well, my love is spurious. Do we love spontaneously, naturally? Or do we learn to love? Or both? Or are the nihilists right to laugh at such questions. Love, they say, is the name we give to our mutually agreed-upon relationships to secure our species and meet our needs for pleasure, comfort, and community. Christians bet their very lives they're wrong.

I like to tell couples I prepare for marriage this little anecdote. Two lovers are having a romantic dinner in a restaurant. They reach across the table and take each other's hands. One says softly, "Thank you for loving me." And then, as if inspired, the other responds, "I couldn't help it." Then I tell the couple to fast-forward twenty-five years. The married couple is having a quiet dinner celebrating their silver anniversary. The husband, remembering a dinner long ago, says, "Thank you for loving me." His wife responds too abruptly, "You're welcome." Both responses—"I couldn't help it" and "You're welcome"—have their truth. We fall in love, we choose to love. So it is with God. We fall in love with the divine mystery. And there are surely times when, bereft of the consolations of faith or faced with heart-breaking loss, we nevertheless choose to love, choose to trust that God is with us.

Don't ask what it means to love my neighbor. I'm too embarrassed to answer. I don't need a calculator to count the times I've passed out sandwiches and coffee to the street people of my city or served meals to families coming to a shelter for the poor. I've seen up close the poor of India and Central America and the cities of America. I haven't turned away. But don't ask me if I have loved them. I could count in seconds my visits to those in jail. Yes, I have visited the sick and hospitalized more than most. But that's what priests do. Do I love my neighbor? Do I love my students? I hope so. I pray for them . . . and that, I believe, is a form of loving.

One of my favorite definitions of love, clearly not the romantic kind, can be traced back to Thomas Aquinas— and no doubt beyond him to Aristotle. Its simplicity and dignity, its rational purity, stop me cold. *To love another is to want what is best for him or her.* If I want what is best for my students, in the sense of wanting what is truly good for them, what is right and just for them, then I love them. If I want what is best for my friends and acquaintances, then I love them. If I want what is best for my enemies, then I love them. And if I want what is best for every living soul on the face of the earth, then I love them. "Love your neighbor as yourself," Jesus tells us. "Want what is best for your neighbor as you want what is best for yourself," might be a loose but still accurate interpretation of the great commandment. To wish absolutely no one ill is no small matter. To wish no one ill, even those who have hurt you deeply, even those who have hurt the ones you love—your spouse, your children, your family, your nation—is no small matter indeed. That kind of wish takes us deep within where we find the grace of God.

What if our Catholic leaders could honestly say, "We wish no other religion ill. We desire what is best for every religion—world religion or regional religion— we desire what is best for every human person?" Our church, somehow, someway, needs to say precisely this. We would be saying that we love all of our brothers and sisters. We would be saying we respect all of our brothers and sisters and their religious traditions. It's what Jesus, I believe, wants us to say. If we could find the courage and humility to utter these words, then the scandalous divisions in the Christian family might have a chance to heal. Ecumenism and interfaith initiatives, stalled in recent decades by a fearful Catholic hierarchy, might find fresh life. And the bitter culture wars within the Catholic communion might be softened with the balm of charity.

What if our nation, building on Abraham Lincoln's "malice toward none," could honestly say, "We wish no other nation, no other people, ill. We desire what is right and just for every nation, for every people—even those whose way of life, whose form of government, appear inimical to ours, even those whom we see as a threat to our national interests?" Imagine that. Voices, I'm sure, would rise immediately to decry such "love" as naïve, unreal, and a threat to our national security. I think just the opposite.

I *must* think the opposite. Otherwise, my faith in God—and as a Christian, my faith in the Gospel—is but my personal spiritual path leading to my personal salvation. When that's the case, the secular spirit of our age, which has so marginalized religious faith as purely a private matter for anxious, superstitious do-gooders, will have strengthened its hegemony over the collective American soul.

This is why Christ's unequivocal call to love, to unconditionally want what is best for others, is revolutionary—and dangerous. That is why we instinctively blunt its meaning and dilute its strength until it rests on some other-worldly pinnacle. Just another ideal. We bow to it, of course, and proceed to ignore it. How can we do other? Let's get real, we tell ourselves. And here we are masters of deceit. For Jesus' call to love indirectly challenges our certainties and absolutes while sowing seeds of relativism. It challenges our deeply rooted feelings of supremacy, of our singular destiny to be the only true beacon of liberty, of our growing spirit of exceptionalism. It's dangerous, all right. It's dangerous because most of the time we want what is best for our own kind. And we are willing to use violence against those we judge as threats to our own best interests. And we are most ready to use violence against our very own if they, like

Jesus, call us to work for justice and right order for all of God's people. Here I'm thinking of the church's spiritual violence against those who don't believe "correctly." And it wasn't so long ago that the physical violence of torture and the stake were inflicted on men and women who didn't believe correctly. The unspeakably brutal religious wars of the sixteenth and seventeenth centuries have taught us nothing; nor has our church's long history of violence against non-Christians.

OF THESE THREE VIRTUES, perhaps only hope isn't dangerous. Yet hope, too, is dangerous because it sustains faith and encourages love. And where there's faith, that is trust, in the loving plan of God and where there is love, that is, wanting what is best for others, there we find the whispers of Gospel revolution leading to the Reign of God. It seems to me, though, that we want the Reign of God on our own terms. We want a Reign of God that will go easy on our racism, classism, sexism, and compulsive consumerism. We want a Reign of God that will understand that our real trust, more often than not, is in our military and political and economic might. No major changes, please. Just some minor tinkering, some fine tuning that might inch us along to God's Reign.

But who am I to entertain such critical thoughts? I confess Dorothy Day leaves me uncomfortable and anxious. She takes the Gospel all too seriously. So does Mother Teresa. So does Gustavo Gutiérrez. So does

Pax Christi. So do sisters, priests, and laity who work with the poorest of the poor and battered women and children. I'm afraid I, too, have made my peace with a domesticated Reign of God. In spite of my troubled conscience—my "conjectures of a guilty bystander"—I claim a place in this imperfect, but Spirit-filled church.

FAITH'S DANGER, I SEE MORE and more clearly, lies in our tendency to codify our mysterious, graced communion with the divine into formulaic prescriptions that demand absolute, unquestioning acceptance by the faithful. The revealed core of our beliefs, of course, is essential in defining the identity and cohesive character of Christianity. We hold fast to our faith tradition that Jesus is the Son of God, that the Spirit dwells in our midst, that God is triune, that we encounter Christ in the sacraments. But failing to grasp, for example, the theological significance of *homoousios*—describing the relationship of God to Jesus in terms of "same substance"—should not be cause for an investigation by the Congregation for the Doctrine of the Faith. Yet insistence on absolute doctrinal conformity is ever more inquisitional and CDF investigations of theologians, clergy, and religious daring to think and write creatively about contemporary issues in Catholic Christianity multiply like untreated cancer cells.

When we stray from the path of Christ, the Way of the Gospel, we become a tight-fisted church so fearful for its integrity and unity and purity that we are willing to prosecute and purge our own members who dare to embrace and engage her organic, evolving, life-giving spirit of grace and freedom in the theological enterprise. In my darker days, I think the church really doesn't want theologians—it wants apologists.

But today the church's sanctuary curtain of secrecy and clerical privilege has been raised just high enough for all to see that underneath the veneer of its passion for orthodoxy lies a subconscious passion for power and control. Inevitably, faith, understood here as assent to church teachings, becomes a tight-fisted command for doctrinal uniformity rather than an open-handed invitation to trust in the divine mystery that, like a magnet, spontaneously draws us, and others, to join in the "serious conversation leading to blessed communion."

COMMUNION

LIKE A PSALM REFRAIN AT VESPERS, Walter Brueggemann's cryptic jewel, "What we are about is serious conversation leading to blessed communion," echoes throughout the first section of this journal.

I'm drawn to it like a magnet because if Christianity is about anything, it is about communion—communion with God, with family and friends, with creation, with mystery. It's the existential dimension to Jesus' Reign of God. We are held, by the Word of God—"serious conversation"—in an unspeakable unity with the whole of creation and its divine source. But this noble truth is but a noble lie to many today. When I preach of communion and intimacy, I preach to ears that often know more of alienation and estrangement than communion and intimacy, to ears that know more of betrayal and heartbreak than the comfort of human solidarity. Maybe what we really are about, the contrarian voices say, is "spurious conversation leading to a cursed alienation."

Evidence in support of the noble lie weighs heavy on me at times. But it is far from the darkest of my doubts. That's because I've had my Emmaus moments, moments of graced communion that leave me a struggling believer, but believer nonetheless, in the mystery of communion. These moments welled up as minor transfigurations. In the grasp of serious conversation and with hearts burning within, doubt disappeared as a mantle of intimacy seemed to wrap itself around each of us who sat at table. The conversation was easy and spontaneous as if in harmony with the very Word of God. We spoke of things that really mattered, of things that mattered most. We lost track of time and place. There was a pull to remain at table, to abide fully in the gifted moment given to us. The serious conversation, our unspoken faith in the hidden presence of the divine, evoked a shared sense of communion.

And then there were those moments at the Eucharistic table when I could almost feel the presence of the Christ as we listened with a single ear to the living word, spoke a prayer of grateful praise, ate a morsel of holy food and sipped a bit of sacred drink. Holy Communion! Not every Mass was an Emmaus moment but many of them were—and are. I think of Dorothy Day's deep sense of communion when she said she could put up with anything between Eucharists.

Something serious and, to me, mysterious has occurred since my ordination in 1965. A half century ago more than 70 percent of Catholics went to weekly Mass. Today that percentage is far less than a third. And in Italy, France, Belgium, and other "Catholic" countries of Europe, the percentage of the faithful celebrating weekly

Mass is in the single digits. Somehow the experience of communion has been diminished or worse. Catholics report they can't take the dreary preaching, poor music, the archaic, stuffy language of the new Missal. And they no longer fear they have committed a mortal sin by missing Mass.

We've used "mortal sin" as a sharp nudge, a threat of eternal punishment, to get Catholics to do what was thought good and necessary for their spiritual lives and eternal salvation—and, it must be said, for the hierarchy's own ability to command and control. For us priests, fail to pray the breviary—mortal sin. Until the late '60s, eat meat on Friday—mortal sin. Fail to make your Easter duty—mortal sin. Practice artificial birth control—mortal sin. A deliberate sexual thought, fantasy, or desire—mortal sin. In high school, my classmates and I were told it was a mortal sin to "go steady," for we were placing ourselves in a near occasion of sin, which it turned out was a sin in itself. I remember as a very young man wishing I were Protestant rather than Catholic. Their moral burdens seemed lighter to me, unaccompanied by the penalty of mortal sin. I found Catholic adolescence a moral minefield. And for those with sensitive consciences, the absolute moral terror of an eternity in hell robbed them of the joy of young life and young love. We confessors know that this crippling fear of an eternity in hell has stunted the religious maturity of countless adults and remains a root cause of serious psychological suffering.

Few today deny the reality of sin, both the garden variety—cutting remarks and the like—and the sin that smothers the spirit and leaves the sinner estranged from the love of God. The occasions of deadly sin are real, we know. Genocide, murder, rape, abuse of children and spouses, violence, greed—the list is long. Long enough that we shouldn't be in the business of "creating" mortal sins like missing Mass on a single Sunday or looking twice at your neighbor's wife. I wonder if the majority of Catholics who don't go to Mass each Sunday crawl into bed at night thinking they are in the state of mortal sin. No, I don't wonder. I think I know.

Most bishops, it seems to me, haven't caught on yet that they can no longer cow Catholics with the threat of mortal sin. Even the threat of excommunication has lost its sting. This isn't to say that Catholics lack a healthy sense of sin. But declarations by church authorities of the moral gravity of sins relating to skipping Mass and much of human sexual behavior increasingly fall on deaf ears. Catholics, perhaps the majority of Catholics, have come to trust in their personal communion with God when they strive to live lives in accord with the Gospel and their consciences. This turn in the Catholic imagination—how the faithful now imagine God as more loving than judging, more merciful than severe—concerns Vatican officials who warn that souls are in grave danger. Such a Catholic imagination, they fear, will inevitably lead to moral laxity and doctrinal confusion. It's interpreted as yet another symptom of the radical secularism and relativism fracturing European and American society. Their anxiety rises when they hear the West described as "post-Christian" and historians announcing the final collapse of religious belief in modern Europe. The historians may be right. But I can hardly imagine we are witnessing the collapse of faith—as distinct from belief—in Europe or elsewhere.

I know little more than the media reports of the deep and complex problems gripping Europe, though I do know Europe, like most of the West, is in a state of crisis—economic, political, social, and religious—and, whether it knows it or not, needs a word from the leadership of the church. I mean here from the Vatican and from the church's bishops. But what it hears is less a word of wisdom drawn from the Gospel and the church's rich intellectual heritage than warnings about the dangers of relativism and secularism. What the leaders of Europe need to hear from the leaders of the church is a fraternal call to work together for the common good of all peoples. Europe's leaders need to hear of the church's blueprint for economic justice, its profound teachings on human dignity that ring true today as in the past. What they hear instead is a lament on the passing of

Christendom and the loss of Europe's Christian character. Fair enough. For what is being lost is profound. Under the pressure of modernity and growing religious pluralism, the symbol system tenuously holding a once common religious imagination continues to melt. And with it goes the church's reconciling mission to inspire a broad commitment to the common good. Perhaps the papacy's most daunting challenge is to evoke a prophetic imagination that would allow the light and wisdom of the Gospel to be a humble yet clear voice for justice and peace. A defensive and aloof critique of our fractured, chaotic, modern world is of no help at all.

We should pay attention to Europe. We should pay particular attention to the single-digit Mass attendance percentages in Europe's traditionally Catholic countries and to serious, informed commentators who announce matter-of-factly the final collapse of religious belief there. Often what happens in Europe comes to pass in America a generation or so later.

So I wonder, does the papacy have the credibility to be heard let alone to be taken seriously in these matters? Can a fractured church speak words of wisdom and hope to a fractured, divided world? Can a church unwilling to critique itself offer constructive criticism to those outside its communion?

And can the papacy even speak to its own? Can it speak to the countless Catholics who feel little if any communion with bishops who have grossly exacerbated the abuse scandals that have shaken the church to its foundations? Can Catholics trust bishops who remain, like medieval princes, free of accountability and responsibility—church or civil? Can the Vatican hold in communion a largely disillusioned and discouraged faithful now numb to reports of the sexual and financial crimes of their priests and bishops? What do Catholics hear today? They hear of Vatican investigations of seminaries and religious women. They hear of theologians being censured for works highly esteemed by their colleagues. They hear of the Leadership Conference of Women Religious stripped of its rightful autonomy and placed under the control of bishops. They hear an insistence on dogmatic and doctrinal orthodoxy that smothers honest thinking and intelligent questions relating to the pastoral and sacramental life of the church. What many Catholics want to hear today is an invitation to be heard. On this matter they hear not a word.

———•◆•———

Everything is connected, and the web is holy.

— Marcus Aurelius

THE CHURCH, OF COURSE, asks us to believe in communion, that God holds us—all of creation, fourteen billion years' worth—in the palm of his hand. The metaphor hints at the unifying force of God's breath, God's force field of energy we call Spirit. If one has been grasped by the Spirit, one has enough evidence to trust that communion can be real. This was the experience of the early Christians who followed the Way of Jesus. This was the experience of saints and mystics, of bishops and preachers, and the ordinary men and women of God who have held the church in unity throughout its long history. Without this deep-felt experience of communion, faith morphs into an uncritical, unthinking intellectual assent to dogmas, doctrines, and disciplines—barren truth without life-giving soul. We have enough of the former, and we thirst for the latter.

Intimacy and Transcendence

YEARS AGO, AS A YOUNG PRIEST confronting the realities of celibate living outside the walls of the seminary, I realized I needed to taste two fundamental experiences to survive both humanly and spiritually. (Yes, I know that what is truly human is spiritual and what is authentically spiritual is always grounded in the human.) My soul longed—forgive this melodramatic language—for regular experiences of intimacy and transcendence. Without these two ego-collapsing and soul-lifting "out of time" moments, I tended to wither as a human being and as a Christian. With them, I not only survived, I tended to flourish. And drawing on their energy, I had the ability to be a "beneficial presence"—a healing witness to the Reign of God. That's our common destiny as Christians: to allow the Christ in us to render us beneficial. Here "Just to be is a blessing" becomes "Just to be, blesses." Leon Bloy put it this way: "God's glory is man [and woman] fully alive." Yes, God's glory is manifested when we humans, we broken vessels, flourish. God takes pleasure when we radiate Christ's peace, when we trust in the goodness of creation even when we come face to face with the tragic dimension of life, the darkness of which often overwhelms us.

In the Oscar-winning film, *Chariots of Fire*, the actor playing the British Olympic sprinter, Eric Liddell, says humbly, "When I run, I feel God's pleasure." That's the communion I'm talking about. When we live in God's grace, when we give Christ's spirit room to abide in our hearts, that's when we non-Olympians experience—at least from time to time—"God's pleasure." It's a fresh metaphor for Christ's peace, Christ's joy—the living presence holding us in communion.

THE SEED OF COMMUNION, COMMUNION'S sacrament, so to speak, is encounter. But I'm thinking now of encounter as intimacy. I should be careful here. Intimacy—it's such a tricky word with its clear subtext of sexual intercourse. While I don't exclude the transporting ecstasy of sexual intercourse, I use the term primarily in a nonsexual sense here. I'm thinking of the kind of intense connectedness that allows the ego-self to slip out of self- awareness. Here we're not thinking of time or place, though we're very much in the present moment. Caught up in this blessing of intense communion, we discover what Thomas Merton and others identify as the *true self*. The true self, the spiritual masters note, is not distracted with questions of identity or status, nor is it anxious or fearful. The true self opens like a flower in the light of authentic human intimacy. And authentic human intimacy is pure communion. I should mention here that the opposite of the true self is the ego-self, or the false self. This is the self that instinctively wonders "how am I doing?" It compares, connives, gossips, backbites, and judges. It's the self that, starved for intimacy, lives a two-dimensional life that invariably leads to a deadening boredom. This self never feels God's pleasure. And the pleasure it does feel is fleeting and deceptive.

Like faith, there is no possibility of true human intimacy without trust. For intimacy requires that we stand before another without our usual defenses and masks, vulnerable yet unafraid. In this graced space we not only find the freedom to reveal our deepest fears and anxieties, but rather what is even more personal, our deepest ideals and dreams, the noblest thoughts of our souls. This trust to stand before another without the armor of our defenses is itself a mystery. For many it's sheer foolishness. But if it is sheer foolishness, then love itself is sheer foolishness. To the contrary, I insist that married or single, young or old, we humans need a few people in our lives, perhaps only one, with whom we are or might become soulmates. I write this with the suspicion that the tears of the lonely can easily dampen the laughter of the merry. While the intimacy of the married can be exquisite, the loneliness of the married can be unspeakably cruel. The Beatles told us to "look at all the lonely people." We can hardly miss them. They live alone. They live on the streets. They live in houses that are prisons where family members live in "solitary confinement." So, maybe it's the capacity for intimacy that is critical. At the heart of the Gospel is a subtext that whispers we are not alone, that our creator has planted in our true selves a capacity for intimacy with God, creation, others—and ourselves. Though we ordinarily discover the blessing of intimacy in and through human relationships, I'm convinced there are countless souls that have been touched by God's affection, God's grace, in such a manner that they have *experienced* the intimacy their souls desire.

Roughly half the world's population of almost seven billion isn't married. If this is an individual's situation, the gift of real "give-you-the-shirt-off-my-back" friendship is one of the few things that matters most. In fact, Jesus takes it a giant step further. If you have a friend that would lay down his or her life for you, you might well weep in gratitude. And then, of course, face the raw question: for whom would I lay down my life?

What happens when celibate priests ask themselves that very question? Who would I lay down my life for? My family? I hope so. Dear friends? I hope so. How about the small number of friends who, by their enduring love and loyalty, have sustained us in the mandated celibacy—mandated loneliness—of priesthood? I give thanks for my friends who have done this for me—contemplative nuns, apostolic sisters, married men and women who have stayed the course with me for almost fifty years. They and my family and my priest friends have lifted me up when I felt I couldn't go on.

AND LIKE ALMOST EVERYTHING in life that is important, intimacy can't be forced. But we need to do more than simply wait for it. We prepare for the communion of intimacy on our knees, so to speak. Authentic intimacy eludes the arrogant and smug, the self-righteous and respectable, the humorless and miserly. But if we live as honestly and humbly as we can, all the while trusting in the abiding presence of God, in one way or another, sooner or later, the divine mystery enters in where no one can see and stays for a while. It's then that we feel God's pleasure.

> It is vain to affirm that which the heart
> does not confirm.
>
> — Aleksandr Solzhenitsyn

TRANSCENDENCE, AS UNDERSTOOD HERE, is no less difficult to describe than intimacy. But such is the case with all spiritual and existential experiences and phenomena. That's why we have collapsed faith into dogma. We can measure compliance to dogma and doctrine, but it remains difficult to take the measure of faith (trust), hope, and love. In the matter of belief, as I've noted above, the church has turned to oaths of fidelity and inquisitions into the orthodoxy of theologians. But in the matter of faith, hope, and love, measurement fails. How truly do you believe? How deeply do you love? How authentic is your hope? All useless questions. Poetry, no doubt, comes closest in these matters. Still, for what they're worth, some thoughts on transcendence, the kissing cousin to intimacy.

I refer here to those elusive moments in which we experience, literally, an unspeakable, harmonious, liberating communion with creation itself. Here, too, the ego-self recedes; time is suspended; and the power of being breaks through ordinary, pedestrian consciousness. Think of the feeling of awe and wonder that comes over someone standing still beneath a panorama of distant stars on a cloudless night. Think of the power of ritual, both religious and secular, to transport us into a realm of ecstasy and communion where, at least for a short time, we escape the banality and routine of our mostly two-dimensional lives. Caught and lifted up by the grace of transcendence, we often feel—to the extent of our remaining ego consciousness—both the smallness of the self and a transforming connectedness. We *belong*! Finite though we are, we exist in a marvelous, mysterious communion with the infinite, with divinity itself. In these moments we see clearly that religion is so much more than orthodox belief and righteous behavior. Here the church's instinct for inquisitions, censures, condemnations, and excommunications appears small and graceless— an infidelity to the transforming power of the Gospel and to the Spirit loose in the world.

The ritual, symbolic richness of the church's sacramental life has the potential to meet the human need for experiences of transcendence. Certainly not always, but often enough in vibrant communities of faith, when the Word of God is preached and heard in the power of the Spirit, time ceases, and the assembly tastes the glory of God's presence and feels God's pleasure. Ask parishioners who have had this experience why they go to Mass and you won't hear, "Because it's a mortal sin to miss Mass on Sunday." You are more likely to hear something like this: "Because I cannot, not go to Mass. Sometimes when I'm at Mass something happens. I'm caught up in something bigger than myself." Experiences of transcendence transform. It's as simple and as complicated as that. Playwright Peter Shaffer put it this way in his play *Equus*: "Without worship, you shrink; it's as brutal as that."

If transcendence transforms, so does intimacy. I need to repeat that I'm referring to experiences of graced intimacy, authentic intimacy that is always, at bottom, a gift. The kind that take us by surprise, that silently converts our anxious vulnerability into a deep sense of bliss where self-doubt disappears, giving way to a blessed communion. When lovers experience this, they instinctively know their lovemaking is holy. For those who live alone, there are occasions when the power of soulmate friendship, even when great distances intervene, transforms their separateness into blessed communion. And they instinctively understand their friendship to be holy. Transformation, after all, is what Jesus preached and taught. The Reign of God is within. Turn away from our vain self-seeking, from what we call sin, and trust that Jesus is the Christ in whose love we find healing and wholeness and communion—salvation.

I'VE SAID THAT INTIMACY AND transcendence are kissing cousins. That was, I now see, an understatement. The relationship is much closer than that. A better metaphor would be to see them as two sides of a single coin. If you have one, you have the other. And if you don't have one, you don't have the other. Every authentic experience of transcendence—alone in a night field with silver stars seeming to be in reach or in the midst of a multitude transported by the power of ritual—is simultaneously an experience of intimacy with creation and its maker. A moment of blessed communion. Likewise, in every experience of authentic intimacy, what Martin Buber describes as an "I-Thou" moment, we sense that we have no real enemies, that the human condition we share has a binding power that connects us, somehow, with the human family. And we want what is best for others, for all others. And the moment of intimacy becomes a moment of blessed communion with the companion we are with and with persons everywhere.

The grace of salvation carries with it the capacity for regular experiences of intimacy and transcendence. And this capacity is a capacity for both. An individual incapable of human intimacy has a soul too small for the ecstasy of transcendence. For those incapable of awe and wonder at the glory of a sunset at sea, the spark of soul needed for intimacy remains too feeble to erupt into flame.

IF I'M RIGHT ABOUT OUR need for regular (what "regular" means will vary from individual to individual and is often influenced by temperament and personality) experiences of intimacy and transcendence, then I can understand why pseudo forms of intimacy and transcendence are so widespread and so frighteningly addictive. Vicarious intimacy—from sexual behaviors devoid of relationship to anonymous Internet chat rooms to the

Facebook phenomenon—touches our deep need for authentic intimacy. But it never delivers—at least the kind of intimacy that transforms and leads to communion. And this need to escape from the routine and numbing rounds of daily work and private life, planted so deep that we can't name it for what it truly is, is therefore met in many cases by the artificial euphoria of illicit drugs or the consciousness-bending effect of intoxication. These chemically induced, pseudo states of transcendence spiral us down to the darkest regions of alienation and estrangement where any promise of communion is mocked as absurd. For others, the escape from the monotony of two-dimensional life is the equally seductive pull of the world of consumption. Shopping temporally wards off everyday depression—the blues—and numbs the superficiality of much of modern life.

In Leonard Bernstein's rock opera *Mass,* the chorus sings, "What I have I don't need / What I need I don't own / What I own I don't want / What I want, Lord, I don't know. / No, no, no, I don't know." What we want, whether we realize it or not, is authentic communion. And the communion under discussion here is born of authentic experiences of intimacy and transcendence— the only experiences that are capable of cracking the superficial shell of consumerist life in the First World.

FOR MANY TODAY, THE WAY OF JESUS, his invitation to intimate friendship and the promise of "New Being" is just too good to be true. When that is the case there is nothing else to do but to pursue the bountiful ersatz forms of intimacy and transcendence that always, inevitably disappoint—and sometimes destroy.

But our tradition insists it is not too good to be true. In John's Gospel Jesus speaks of an indwelling intimacy: "Live on in me, as I do in you. . . . I am the vine, you are the branches." Followers of Christ learn how to step "outside of time" in the new order he called the Reign of God. But we have to sit down, sit still, and trust that he is present. It can take for many of us close to a lifetime. This faith in the transforming power of Christ, the spiritual masters tell us, is God's ultimate, intimate gift and our only hope.

Authority and Communion

GROWING UP IN CLEVELAND IN POST–World War II America, I realize now that I had a number of things going for me that gave me a sense of communal identity. Beyond my family, deeply entrenched in its Catholic world made flesh in Holy Name parish and its revered pastors, my brothers, sister, schoolmates, and I lived our childhood years just before the great suburban expansion. As city dwellers, we bonded by the power of place, sharing a tree-lined neighborhood, a kind of village that bred into us a sense of security and belonging. We played touch football on our faded red brick streets

and knew the names of neighbors who watched from
their front porches. The neighborhood knitted us into
an unspoken social communion while first communions
and confirmations and the great feasts of Christmas and
Easter sowed the seeds of a deep religious communion.
City dwellers though we were, the parish and the neighborhood cradled us in the comforting communion of a
small town or village.

But soon the GI Bill kicked in, and the sons (and a few
daughters) of working-class Catholics went off to college
where they learned to think as adults and master the skills
necessary for their entrance into the professions. Profes-
sional success led to modest yet previously unheard-of
salaries, and the migration to the suburbs proved irresist-
ible to the majority of my neighbors. In most cases, the
sense of community grounded in compact neighborhoods
was lost. And, arguably, much more. A secular mind-set
settled over suburban America that challenged the unquestioned values of the tight-knit Catholic parishes of
the pre-1960s. There were clear advantages to the new
life away from the ageing streets and buildings of the city.
And many of the suburban parishes flourished, nurturing
strong and vital Catholic communities. But a new way of
thinking accompanied the city pilgrims to the airy streets
of second- and third-ring suburbia. And the new way of
thinking—and living—was not always conducive to a
sense of social communion and religious practice.

The scholar Alan Ehrenhalt caught some of the main threads of this new way of thinking in his study of mid-twentieth-century Chicago.

> Most of us in America believe a few simple prop-ositions that seem so clear and self-evident they scarcely need to be said. Choice is a good thing in life, and the more of it we have, the happier we are. Authority is inherently suspect; nobody should have the right to tell others what to think or how to behave. Sin isn't personal, it's social; individual human beings are creatures of the so-ciety they live in.[11]

Our spiritual elders might comment, of course, that choice is good, but only when we choose amongst a num-ber of "goods." We don't have a choice when it comes to stealing or not, assaulting another or not, killing or not. (I know moral choice is far more complicated than sim-ply choosing one good over other goods. The explod-ing field of bioethics alone makes that crystal clear.) The saints remind us that happiness is an elusive quality of soul. We are happy when we forget about the pursuit of our own happiness and live in such a way that we con-tribute to the happiness and well-being of others—when we want what is best for others. Happiness, like all the really important things in life, should never be pursued directly. When that's the case, there is always too much ego involved for real happiness to emerge. Placing uncritical choice on the pedestal of freedom only reinforces the radical individualism that weakens social cohesion and religious communion. But our elders' greatest anxiety would be rooted in what Ehrenhalt had to say about our deep-seated suspicion of authority.

We have good reason to be wary of authority. Lord John Acton, sensing the real and profound danger inherent in the First Vatican Council's declaration of papal infallibility, gave us one of the most quoted axioms of modern times: *Power tends to corrupt, and absolute power corrupts absolutely.* We can trace the church's great sins in both straight and crooked lines back to abuses of authority—to her unholy compulsion for "command and control." As a young priest, I devoured the Jesuit John L. McKenzie's *Authority in the Church.* I learned from him that the authority in the church should be modeled on the authority of Jesus. "The New Testament," McKenzie writes, "is anti-authoritarian in a proper sense. It abhors the type of domination which in the New Testament world was seen in secular power or in religious autocracy. It is anti-authoritarian in the sense that it permits no member of the Church to occupy a position of dignity and eminence; the first in the Church must be the . . . slave of others, and may strive for no dignity and eminence except in dedication to service in love."[12] Church authority is meant to sustain the order necessary for the church to carry out its mission. It's meant to be a minimalist authority grounded in the spiritual freedom Jesus preached throughout his ministry.

It's naïve to think we can live without authority. Still, we're tempted to try to do just that—to live without authority. Especially we Americans who live in the land of the free. So I suspect sleeping seeds of the anarchist lie buried deep in the American breast. Ehrenhalt was correct to assert that in America, authority is inherently suspect. And that should give us pause. Paul Tillich, the Lutheran theologian and philosopher, put it this way: "He who tries to live without authority tries to be like God who alone is by Himself. And like everyone who tries to be like God, he is thrown down to self-destruction. Be it a single human being, be it a nation, be it a period of history like our own."

Both Tillich and McKenzie understood the inherent tension between authority and freedom, a tension evident from the earliest days of the church to our postmodern era. But this tension slips back and forth from a healthy life-giving tension into twisted knots of radical authoritarianism or radical individualism. In either extreme, communion is ruptured and we lose sight of the truth that the most enduring safeguard of authority is not power, but freedom. We pilgrims, especially our shepherds, are still learning this lesson.

For me it comes down to this—the purpose of religious authority is to hold us in communion with God, each other, and creation itself. It achieves this goal of communion primarily through witness to the liberating power of the Gospel paradox—life through death, fulfillment in service, strength through surrender, peace in nonjudgmental acceptance of others. This witness is hardly passive, although it begins with the authoritative witness of the authentic church leader. It is found in the prophetic preaching of the bishop and presbyter and layperson. It is observed in the religious educator who tells the story of Jesus and his way of the kingdom so compellingly that her students sense their own dignity as part of a people of faith. It's found in theologians whose books deepen our faith and liberate our spirits and encourage us to reflect on our lives through the lens of our faith tradition. Church authorities hold us in communion when they honor our tradition, our past, by calling us to live freely in the present as God's beloved. They hold us in communion by repeating again and again the invitation to build the City of God by fostering the *commonweal* rather than the tight-fisted hold on what serves as one's private good.

So, the church's ordained authorities are first witnesses, preachers, and teachers who understand that they themselves must ring true as persons of faith. When that's the case, they will know, almost by instinct, how to order their local faith community. Authority maintains communion by ensuring the order necessary for right relationships, that is, for communion. It's right for church authorities to remind us that Christians are not religious freelancers but members of God's family, what we call the communion of saints. Included in this ordering is the discernment of charisms so that the communion, the *communio*, will be sustained by appropriate pastoral care and preaching. Seen in this light, church authority is best understood as a minimalist authority. That's something we haven't seen since Constantine's official underwriting of the early church. Now we have not only infallible popes but a "creeping infallibility" that only makes worse the present crisis of authority.

Echoing St. Augustine, Pope John XXIII gave us a maxim especially relevant for our own day: "In necessary things, unity; in doubtful matters, freedom; in all things, charity." The trouble is that only the Vatican believes it knows what is necessary; the same Vatican that sees very little relating to faith and morals that is doubtful. I can't remember a church official addressing a complex bioethical issue, for example, saying something like, "This is a complex question, and we don't have a position on the matter at this time." And wouldn't it be wonderful if the official added, "We look forward to cooperating with bio-ethicists outside the Catholic tradition to determine the underlying moral implications of this issue." And when it comes to charity . . . whose charity? The meanness evident in the censures leveled at American theologians Elizabeth Johnson and Margaret Farley, among others, were no doubt thought by those issuing them to be "charitable," good and necessary for the well-being of the church.

AS WE'VE SEEN, WHEN AUTHORITY isn't authoritative, it confuses uniformity with unity and soon prizes doctrinal orthodoxy and moral rectitude over interior faith, hope, and love. When authority isn't authoritative, it stands ready to do the opposite of holding the faithful in communion—it stands ready to excommunicate. When authority isn't authoritative, it comes across as arrogant—authority's fatal flaw. There isn't the slightest hint in the Gospels that Jesus displayed signs of arrogance. Yet, we hear of our bishops described as arrogant. Flannery O'Connor was right. "Smugness is the great Catholic sin." But we find smugness—self-righteousness, triumphalism, patriarchy, arrogance—not only in our church prelates, we see its traces in ourselves if we but look deeply enough. Our tragic culture wars, rooted in dogma hardened into ideology, make this clear, for ideologies are by definition smug. And so our own strains of smugness need to be challenged by the voice of authentic authority as well as by our sisters and brothers in faith. Consider this challenge to the smug clericalism of more than a few clergy: most churches have a separate door leading to the sacristy used primarily by the priest. What if we placed a sign above our sacristy doors that read, "Servants' Entrance"?

The Unseen Order

THERE ISN'T A CLASS I TEACH AT the university where I fail to mention the inspired insight of William James, America's pioneering psychologist and philosopher. "There is," James insists, "an unseen order, and our supreme good is to be found in living in harmony with this order." The agnostics in class lean forward sensing that this could be important for their first steps outside of religious belief. What does James mean, a student will ask, by "unseen order"? James doesn't tell us. He doesn't even try. The nature of this unseen order remains elusive. Most of the Catholics in the class connect it with God's will or God's plan for us. A few will see a connection with the Gospel. Some will connect it with the rhythms of the universe or traditional natural law theory.

Most of the students do a little mental wrestling with the unseen order. The agnostics, while they aren't sure about the existence of God, want to hear more about this mysterious order—especially if their "supreme good" depends on it. A few suspect I'm setting them up to announce that God is the unseen order. What James does so creatively is to raise the question that most thinking people ask: is there some order, some law, some plan, some truth outside myself that I should attend to? Or are we each, in our splendid, horrifying individuality, a law unto ourselves? I've talked to students who have tried to live that way—throwing off all authority—only to discover a confounding state of alienation and estrangement, a brand of nihilism that draws them gradually and relentlessly into a life without wonder or enchantment. For some budding agnostics, thinking about this enigmatic "order" prompts them to see religious faith and belief in a new light.

But the golden kernel of James' insight is his use of the word "harmony." "[O]ur supreme good is to be found in living in *harmony* with this order." Not in obedience to it, not in surrender to it, not in submission to it—but in harmony with it. James evokes here the "music of the spheres." When we live in harmony with the Holy Spirit we glimpse or "hear" the holy communion of the Reign of God that vibrates with the energy we call love. That's why the mystics can say that Christianity is not a law to be obeyed, but a presence to be grasped. And when the presence is grasped, transformation and communion follow, inevitably. Christian living then is not so much obedience but much more a staying in tune with the Gospel. And when we are not in tune, when we fall out of harmony with the unseen order, we experience discord. (Discord is too weak a word for the injustice and violence of our world, but it's apt for capturing the shrill attacks of the culture warriors of church and politics.)

But discord sooner or later evokes its opposite—harmony. I'm thinking here of Jesus' great gift—peace. He gives us a peace, a state of harmony and communion that the world cannot give. Harmony evokes a realization of different notes held in a state of communion—different notes held in a state of grace that descend on their listeners as "blessed communion."

James doesn't tell us what our "supreme good" is. For the agnostic, it must consist of a general sense of well-being—good health; sufficient wealth; a measure of happiness that follows upon moral rectitude, civil responsibility, and an inbred sense of patriotism for the common good. But for the person of faith, the "supreme good" is new life in Christ; it is communion; it is what we Christians call salvation.

IMAGINE A CHURCH THAT CONSISTENTLY offered an invitation to live in harmony with the Gospel rather than solemn declarations of what is true or false, what is right or wrong, or who is in and who is out. Imagine a church that trusted in the fundamental goodness of God's creation rather than asserting its authority to correct and condemn. Imagine a church that before judging the world by the light of the Gospel, judged itself by that same light. Imagine a church that recognized that the Spirit is the source and substance of our communion rather than canons and catechisms.

For followers of Jesus, the unseen order is the Reign of God, and it's God's grace that holds us in harmony. And when we are held in this "state of harmony," this "state of grace," we experience Jesus' peace, and we discover in our heart of hearts, to our immense joy, that God wills our supreme good.

> No sacrifice needed; no religion, even;
> not good behavior either. God loves
> because God loves, period.

—James Carroll

My Sin against Communion

ON MAY 23, 1965, THE DAY after my ordination, I walked into the kitchen of my parents' home an hour or so before my first solemn Mass (in Latin with a deacon, subdeacon, and archpriest) at Holy Name Church. Two of my parents' closest friends, Zelda and Gleason, had driven down from central Michigan to be present for my ordination and first Mass. They were our house guests, and as they and my parents and I converged just moments before I left for the church, Gleason said to me, "Zelda and I have been fasting since midnight." They were as joyful and excited as my parents—eagerly looking forward to participating in my first Mass and receiving communion. "We've been fasting since midnight." Those words nearly crushed me. Zelda and Gleason, faithful and practicing Episcopalians intended to receive communion. Episcopalians, like Anglicans, believe in the real presence. I knew this. But I also knew the practice of the church to exclude from communion all who were not in communion with the Roman Catholic Church.

To this day, I find it hard to think of this awkward moment, let alone to write about it. My legalist sacramental theology kicked in and smothered my instinct to think pastorally. I began haltingly, "I'm afraid . . . we don't have intercommunion." Before I could go on, Gleason said to his wife with a weak smile intended to hide his hurt, "He's trying to let us down gently."

I was off to a grand start as a new priest—I had succumbed to the social pressure of my approaching ordination and had taken the oath against modernism, and then I failed to exercise ordinary pastoral judgment and invite my parents' friends to receive communion at my first Mass. And this in less than twenty-four hours as a priest. What had the seminary done to me? Some would say I was a good priest here. Communion is for Catholics after all. Catholics who are in the state of grace, Catholics who don't practice birth control, Catholics who go to Mass each Sunday. What had the seminary done to me? I still ask that question almost fifty years after my ordination. I know priests who feel they need only two books on their desks—the *Code of Canon Law* and the *Catechism of the Catholic Church*. These books have their place, of course, but they are not the final word when it comes to the "law" of Christ. I had a lot to learn.

Priests, I believe, are meant to be agents of communion, announcers of God's invitation to God's people to walk with Christ even though we stumble along as wounded, limping sinners. Instead, many of us are enforcers of the code, quick to name sin and slow to name grace. We are quick, too, to point out transgressions of all sorts and slow to see holiness all about us, especially in the lives of ordinary good people. "Thou shalt not" is our mantra. I'm reminded of the last stanza of William Blake's poem, "Garden of Love": And priests in black gowns were walking their rounds / and binding with briars my joys and desires. God help us. We priests tend to be binders rather than liberators. Like the prophet Isaiah, we have been anointed by the Spirit "to bring glad tidings to the lowly, to heal the brokenhearted, to proclaim liberty to the captives and release to the prisoners."[13] Instead of glad tidings, we announce dire warnings; instead of healing the brokenhearted, we break hearts when we insist on the letter of the law; instead of releasing those held captive by their fear of a punishing God, we tighten their briars and chains with threats of divine punishment. It's easy for preachers to sin against communion. We have to hold in creative harmony God's unconditional love for all of humanity and the tragic human capacity for turning away from this love—and the alienation and estrangement that inevitably follow. In a real sense, theologian Catherine Hilkert writes, preaching is "naming grace." We sin against communion when we ministers of the word condense our preaching to "naming sin."

Breaking Communion

CLEVELAND, LIKE MANY OF THE larger U.S. dioceses, is downsizing big time. In recent years fifty parishes have been closed or merged after years of study, consultation, and planning by diocesan officials, clergy, and laity. Many of the closed or merged parishes simply couldn't go on, and the bishop's decision, though painful to most of the parishioners affected, was defensible. But eleven of the closed parishes cried foul and appealed their termination to the Vatican's Congregation for the Clergy. And to everyone's surprise, the Vatican, citing canonical missteps by the bishop, upheld the parishioners appeal and directed the bishop of Cleveland to reopen the parishes in question.

The reasons for the closings and mergers echoed the explanations of dioceses that earlier had downsized—the shortage of priests, the move of Catholics from the city to the outer suburbs, and the financial burden to the diocese of sustaining parishes unable to meet their own expenses. I'll comment on only one of the causal factors here, the shortage of priests. During my years of teaching at John Carroll University, I asked dozens of men if they had thought about being priests. To my surprise, only one student said that he hadn't thought of it. All the others said they had. And then they added quickly that they wanted to be married and have a family. The priest-shortage rationale is patently thin because the clergy crisis is a church-made crisis. Denying diocesan priests their baptismal right to the sacrament of marriage is weakening the *experience* of communion for countless Catholics. It's clear the growing drop in the number of clergy and their rising average age—now about sixty-five—has serious implications for parish communities. The genius of Catholicism is that it is fundamentally local. Catholics experience communion in the fold of the parish. When church doors are locked, parishioners instinctively understand that the networks of community that supported them as a pilgrim people have been cut. Closing parishes breaks communion. And it is misguided to say downsizing parishes was and is a tragic necessity. It's tragic all right, but it could have been avoided had the celibacy issue been put on the table.

As painful as it is to have one's parish closed, this national phenomenon remains on another level, a symptom of a larger breakdown in Catholic communion. Recent research, I noted earlier, reveals that one out of ten Americans is a former Catholic and that the second largest U.S. religious "denomination" is former Catholics. Vital parishes remain, and there are indeed many, but there are more parishes that leave much to be desired. Of course, the exodus of large numbers of Catholics from their church can't be blamed solely on the parish. The church's woefully underdeveloped, act-focused, medieval theology of human sexuality has to be close to the top of the list. Jostling for position here are the unmet spiritual needs of Catholics; the church's restrictive, subordinating attitude towards women; the absence of real financial transparency; and the shocking sexual abuse scandals and the arrogant episcopal cover-ups that made a terrible reality all the worse. Catholic parents of gay and lesbian sons and daughters, from conservative to centrist to progressive, don't believe for a moment that their offspring are "objectively disordered." One mother of a gay son told me that she was "hanging on by her fingertips" to the church. "The church is telling me my son doesn't have the right to fall in love, that he doesn't have the right to share his life with someone he loves."

No doubt the shift from faith as certitude concerning the church's dogmatic teachings to faith as trust in our enduring covenant with God—a faith that includes ignorance and doubt—is a factor here. So also is the conviction that God's embrace is wider than the Christian faithful, that God is greater than religion. To some immeasurable extent, Catholics no longer fear they will suffer the loss of their souls if they separate themselves from the communion of those Catholics we describe as "practicing." The bishops, of course, haven't caught on. They still see themselves as the only certified brokers of salvation.

And yes, some break the bonds of communion due to a personal crisis of faith, or more commonly, a crisis of belief. But these, I suspect, are the minority of those who walk away from the church or simply "leave in place." Yet, such is the power of God's love that the ties of communion are never definitively cut. Within the fold or without, seekers of every stripe find moments of intimacy and transcendence—rumors of angels, if you will—in art, science, nature, and even the secular city. Some report their spiritual lives are healthy, even flourishing. Others grieve and long for their lost spiritual home. Still others believe they have suffered spiritual violence at the hands of their shepherds. For these individuals and the victims of clergy abuse, community and communion are simply empty words devoid of reality or meaning.

IT'S CLEAR TO ME NOW THAT ALL religions are imperfect and impure. And even sinful. I would be naïve to think otherwise, especially since the Vatican Council insists that the Catholic Church will always be in need of renewal and reform. A sign of healthy religion is that it evokes and fosters at least a subliminal awareness that we are held in communion by the One God who is the source of all that exists. We are one because of our common "creature-hood." From the very beginning, however, most monotheistic religions, through a tragic, misguided intuition, came to believe that the solution to violence was violence—and worse, a violence endorsed by God. And so the very institutions meant to evoke and sustain community became communion breakers.

HEALTHY RELIGION FOSTERS HEALTHY communion—a holy communion. And this holy communion expands outward sensing in sacraments and symbols the Oneness of God that embraces all. It sees truth, goodness, and beauty in spite of the tragic dimension to life. Healthy communion plants seeds of compassion and a thirst for justice while awakening the believer's prophetic imagination.

Sick communions, that is, sick religious communities, insist on boundaries and turn in on themselves with the fervor and passion of the self-righteous. They are quick to excommunicate and generally are wary of "others," of those outside their religious communion. They tend to scapegoat "others," placing on their backs the social and political ills of their time. As ideologues, their religious certainties and certitudes wall them off from dialogue and make them deaf and blind to the voices and actions of those outside their circle. Their fatal flaw is their deeply ingrained inability for any serious self-criticism or self-judgment.

I'm afraid this distinction between healthy and sick communions is too facile, too simplistic. Most religions, most of the time, are healthy *and* sick, pure *and* impure, prophetic *and* cowardly at the same time. They give the neo-atheists of our time ample fodder for their salvos.

My own church can break your heart and heal your soul. It can declare an individual excommunicated and reach out to schismatics. It can project triumphalism and speak for the poor and powerless. It can be rudely authoritarian and quietly magnanimous. It's not always pure and honest and true. It is, nonetheless, my spiritual home and it consistently holds up the Gospel of Christ to me. But I speak here of the "ordering church," the church of bishops and curia and the papacy. My own church is also the community gathered for Eucharist at the Cleveland Carmelite monastery, the students praising God at the 10 pm Sunday Mass on the campus of John Carroll University. My own church is the "coffee house theologians" who meet every Saturday morning. Imperfect, of course. Wounded, without question. At the same time, we are mostly joyful and faithful and grateful.

For we have been held in the one embrace of the Spirit.
We have been marked and transformed by the power of
holy communion.

> Become friends to those who have no friends.
> Become family to those who have no family.
> And become community to those
> who have no community.

— Blessed John Paul II

A Secular Age

YOU MAY RECALL THAT YOU are reading "the spiritual journal of a secular priest." Some might think "secular priest" is an oxymoron. Priests aren't secular, after all; or they shouldn't be. They aren't "worldly." They are men of God who touch the sacred mysteries—make present the Real Presence in consecrated bread and wine, forgive sinners in the name of Christ and the church, preach the Gospel and console the suffering. In this sense, they have long been thought to be "not of this world." Older readers might remember that it was once commonplace to refer to priests who didn't belong to a monastery or to a religious order (e.g., Dominican, Jesuit, Benedictine) as "secular." They lived *in* the world, so to speak, but were not *of* the world. Today secular priests are more commonly identified as "diocesan."

But the writer of this journal is clearly a secular priest. I'm obviously not a monk. You will find no identifying initials after my name (e.g., O.P, S.J., O.S.B.), and I live in an apartment adjacent to the university campus where I work. But the adjective "secular" means more here than to designate what I am not. I am a priest who is both *in* the world and, with no apologies, *of* the world. But I hope my values transcend the materialist and consumerist aspects of much of contemporary life in North America. I don't believe that as a priest I am set apart from others, but rather set in the midst of others where I am called and ordained to be a servant leader, a preacher of the Word that liberates its hearers from the suffocating "unfreedom" of the shallow secular—the moral and ethical confusion—of contemporary society. And I believe I am a man of faith, trusting in the power of the Spirit to live faithfully as a disciple of Christ. But the context of my life is indeed "the world"—the city, the marketplace, the campus, the coffee house. If I am to find holiness and integrity, it is not going to be in a monastery or in a religious community, but here in Cleveland, Ohio, and here in these United States of America in the first years of the twenty-first century. And while the shallow, seductive side of the world presents real dangers, the world remains the playground of "angels" where the divine lies hidden but present in the very ordinariness of individual and common life. Yet the dangers—

narcissism, greed, decadence, power, to name but a few—remain real, erupting as demonic explosions of violence or silently corrupting the soul's integrity. Still, the fathers of the Second Vatican Council proclaimed what our mystics and contemplatives have always known—the world, the secular, is holy as creation is holy. It participates in the oneness of God's creation, which God declared to be good, very good.

IN 2007 THE CANADIAN AND Catholic philosopher, Charles Taylor published an important 874-page book, *The Secular Age*. It's not designed for speed reading or a day at the beach. It is, on the other hand, worthy of careful reading and study.

The secular, for Taylor, is understood from three perspectives. The first is the relatively modern phenomenon that separates religion from public life. We see here the roots of our cherished separation of church and state. The second is the rather sweeping loss of belief that connects with the first section of this journal in which I reflected on the distinction between faith and belief. The collapse or near collapse of religious belief in Europe, the startling single-digit percentage of Mass attendance in Europe's Catholic countries, the struggle for survival of mainline Protestant churches in the United States, the loss of one out of three individuals raised as Catholic here bear witness to this loss of belief. The focus of Taylor's work settles on his third understanding of the secular.

At least in the West, we are faced with a situation un-
heard of before modernity. Multiple and powerful al-
ternate nonreligious scenarios for making sense of life
have established themselves in the modern mind. Taylor
is thinking here of the scientific worldview that promises, for some, answers to the major questions of life
or the focus on individual fulfillment as one's ultimate
concern. The "I'm spiritual but not religious" mentality
is at home in this scenario. Especially in America, the
obsession with success and status can override religious
conviction and practice. The sustaining energy of these
alternative meaning systems is a pseudoauthenticity. It's
an egoism that hides behind slogans like "I've got to be
me" and "I did it my way." We seldom hear even a whisper of community or communion or the common good.

Taylor observes, "The coming of modern secularity
. . . has been coterminous with the rise of a society in
which for the first time in history a purely self-sufficient
humanism came to be a widely available option. I mean
by this a humanism accepting no final goals beyond human flourishing, nor any allegiance to anything else beyond this flourishing. Of no previous society was this
true."[14] If Taylor's read is accurate, and I obviously think
it is, the implications for vital communities and communion, not to mention the future of religion as we understand it today, are mind-boggling. In this sense of the
secular, the Christian belief that we find life to the full

in dying to the ego-self, in compassionate action for the poor and powerless, in building the Reign of God by being men and women for others, seems fanciful at best.

In this light, we shouldn't be surprised that organized religion is in big trouble. Appeals to church authority, once compelling in itself, now fizzle like firecracker duds. Threats of excommunication and damnation cause nary a shiver. And in this light, the drop in church attendance, Catholic and mainline Protestant, is understandable, though regrettable. The pluralism Taylor points to will not go away, and Catholic plodding on as usual along with the disingenuous and deflecting investigations of our seminaries, our theologians, and American sisters is a failure of leadership.

I've turned to Taylor's study of secularism because of secularism's impact on the experience of communion that I see as vital for human flourishing, both personal and spiritual. The radical individualism spawned by this phenomenon, an individualism that looks no further than one's personal fulfillment, stands clearly against the core truths and values of the Gospel. But Taylor's analysis goes deeper. The very conditions of belief, he demonstrates, are changed in our secular society. We have moved "from a society where belief in God is un-challenged and indeed, unproblematic, to one in which it is understood to be one option among others, and fre-quently not the easiest to embrace."[15]

Most of the bishops gathered for the Second Vatican Council grasped this turn to the secular. Most understood that the Christian message and way of life was indeed one option among others and that the great challenge before the church was to awaken the Catholic imagination to discover a new approach—a new language—for the proclamation of Christ's Gospel. *The Church in the Modern World* bravely met this challenge. I still marvel at the freshness of language, the pastoral tone, and the theological astuteness of its opening sentence: "The joys and hopes, the griefs and the anxieties of the men of this age, especially those who are poor or in any way afflicted, these are the joys and hopes, the griefs and anxieties of the followers of Christ." But it appears our church leaders have lost their nerve and more and more of late return to forms and styles of proclamation and discourse that echo the long-lost age of Christendom.

THE SHIFT FROM FAITH AS CERTITUDE to faith as trust means that we are moving beyond the God of dogma to the "God beyond God," a necessary but unnerving "quest for the living God." Dietrich Bonhoeffer asked the right question more than half a century ago, "How do we speak of God without religion? How do we speak in a secular fashion of God?" Rabbi Abraham Heschel gave us a hint when he quipped, "There are no proofs for the existence of God, only witnesses." Just what kind of witnesses are we? And what kind of witness am I?

I've come to see there needs to be witness before words, experience before doctrine. Are we as a church up to that? And what is it we can learn from the witnesses in our secular city? The church and secular society both speak of fulfillment. That might be a good starting point. Here our stories of faith might begin with St. Augustine's confession that our hearts are restless until they rest in God. Also, our stories of faith are stories of community and communion. The spiritual restlessness that stirs in many corners of the secular world and the moral chaos and alienation that lie just below the veneer of contemporary social intercourse make the men and women of our age ready for "serious conversation leading to blessed communion." But is the church ready for such conversation?

Can we imagine religionless belief? Religionless faith? Do we believe that God is bigger than religion? Bigger even than our search for meaning? These are real questions, and on how we answer them hangs the future of the church. In the meantime, we as church need to gear up for conversations with the "minimal religionists" and the legions claiming to be "spiritual but not religious." Their spiritualities appear quite individualistic. Many, I'm convinced, find the circle of our communion more attractive than we might believe. Sadly, we have yet to seize this opportunity for a new spirit of dialogue and proclamation. The turn to the secular has left the church unsteady, defensive, and ever more exclusive. But the church, Taylor reminds us, "is meant to be the place in which human beings, in all their difference and disparate itineraries, come together; and in this regard, we are obviously falling short."[16]

Charles Taylor now and Dietrich Bonhoeffer earlier have alerted us to the challenges to religious faith and communion inherent in our secular age. Both men call us to a conversion of consciousness, to a freeing of our imaginations, in order to strengthen our solidarity as a pilgrim people lighting the way for ourselves and our secular fellow travelers. We shouldn't be surprised, however, that it's Thomas Merton who speaks most powerfully to this conversion of consciousness in which he discovered his deep communion with the human family.

> In Louisville, on the corner of Fourth and Walnut, in the center of the shopping district, I was suddenly overwhelmed with the realization that I loved all these people, that they were mine and I was theirs, that we could not be alien to one another even though we were total strangers . . . I have the immense joy of being human, a member of the race in which God himself became incarnate. As if the sorrows and stupidities

of the human condition could overwhelm me, now that I realize what we all are. If only everybody could realize this! There is no way of telling people that they are all walking around shining like the sun![17]

PRAYER

WHEN IT COMES TO PRAYER there are no professors. Yet I believe I have something to say about prayer even though this section of my journal holds little more than the reflections of a novice. That's quite true in spite of my experience as a preacher, spiritual director, and retreat master. And, I confess, even the rather defensive tone to these opening sentences is itself something I should talk over with a spiritual guide and take to prayer myself. Foolhardy or not, I plunge ahead.

I'm writing here primarily but not exclusively about personal prayer rather than focusing on the communal, public prayer we call liturgy. There are indeed professors, experts if you will, who speak and write about liturgical prayer. Come to think of it, these "professors" are not always experts. I'm thinking here of translators of liturgical texts. The new Roman Missal imposed on the English-speaking Catholic world on the first Sunday of Advent in 2011 is substantially dreadful. It is the worst spiritual stumbling block, save the virtual rescinding of the Second Vatican Council, I've encountered in almost fifty years as a presider. I find myself "reading" the awkward and stiff presider prayers at Mass rather than "praying" them. The Missal is not only a slavishly literal translation of a Latin text, its grammar and syntax hardly ring true to the English-speaking ear. Worse, still, is its exaggerated emphasis on the sacrificial character of worship from an unworthy, worm-like assembly of believers, that Jesus' salvific legacy is not for all but for many, that we can merit God's love.

I've learned a great deal from liturgical theologians and spiritual writers. But even the spiritual masters, especially spiritual masters like Dorothy Day and Thomas Merton, are wise enough not to attempt to teach us how to pray. So what follows does not say much at all about how one might pray or how one should pray. But one thing I do believe, as tricky as prayer is, we are in big trouble if we don't pray. Since prayer as I understand it flows more or less spontaneously from our spiritual life—what I prefer to call our interior life—a substantial portion of this section of the journal will deal with prayer's proper preface: living in harmony with God's unseen order. This state of graced harmony silently draws the one who prays deeper into the Reign of God where he or she learns, without lessons, to live in the presence of God.

———•◆•———

Willfulness vs. Willingness

The first chapter of Gerald May's *Will and Spirit,* is worth the price of the book itself. Hands down, it is one of the most insightful pieces of spiritual and psychological writing I've ever encountered. I believe this chapter, "Willfulness and Willingness," to be essential reading for anyone daring to engage in spiritual direction or pastoral counseling. Here's the gist of it. Nothing of value, no matter how worthy or noble, should be forced. Neither *can* it be forced, though we try nonetheless. Let's begin with the transcendent values of love, beauty, and truth. Most, I assume, would agree that they can't be forced. Neither can friendship, gratitude, humility, hospitality, and especially, worship. It should be clear that authentic prayer can't be forced any more than we can force "spiritual growth." I'm smiling at the cartoon of a man sitting in his pastor's study. "I want to reach spiritual perfection as soon as possible," he says solemnly to the priest across from him. "Then," he adds, "I want to move on to bigger and better things." The parishioner's "just do it" attitude is the epitome of willfulness. We can but wonder what he had in mind as "bigger and better things" to do once he had checked off "spiritual perfection" on his to-do list. May would also argue that the pursuit of "excellence," the *über*-virtue of our day, is regularly ambushed by our sheer willfulness.

Sometimes I think willfulness is America's defining character trait, especially if we are convinced that the object of our willful striving is noble, good, or at least morally neutral. Our nation's rhetoric and actions support the contention that we are ready to willfully impose democracy on sovereign countries whether they desire it or not. But what else can a secular nation appeal to for human progress other than a sustained, determined, unyielding will to achieve our righteous goals and objectives? So, it isn't surprising that many believers take a willful approach to their prayer lives and spiritual lives. Willfulness is in the air we breathe.

OUR CATHOLIC TRADITION, OF COURSE, is wary of willfulness to the point of labeling it heresy. "Spiritual growth" (I prefer the term "spiritual maturation" which avoids the quantitive connotation of "growth") pursued by anyone inattentive to the foundational reality of grace and its essential role in spiritual maturation is flirting with Pelagianism, the heresy that holds human will, if determined and disciplined, can of itself lead the seeker to moral rectitude and holiness. But many of us keep striving, keep trying to grow spiritually as if the whole business of holiness is primarily our doing. May offers some sound advice for those of us willfully trying to do better. He reminds us that willful individuals often are obsessed with *mastery* and *control*—modern "virtues" that can take us only so far and often impede authentic communion and community. It is important, May writes, to counter or at least balance our penchant for mastery and control with the virtues associated with willingness—*trust and surrender*. Individuals who are far more willing than willful understand that the important things in life can't be forced. They *trust* God, they live in harmony with the unseen order. They "surrender," in the sense of the oft-repeated cliché, "It is what it is." Their surrender is but acceptance of reality. My guess is that their blood pressure on average is lower than the blood pressure of willful people, and their stress level is lower too. "Willing" individuals walk the spiritual path side by side with the set-jaw marchers we've described as willful. But it seems to me the willing rather than willful men and women enjoy the journey more.

So it's important not to force prayer. When we simply can't pray, we would be wise to acknowledge that reality, as disturbing as it might be. The danger here is that we won't even sit for prayer, or fail to "say" the prayers we know by heart, which often take us around or through those impasses where prayer seems inauthentic or futile. But wanting to pray, the will to pray, the spiritual masters remind us, is a form of prayer itself. Often in our secular, willful society, stopping for prayer is thought to be a kind of betrayal, a kind of quitting the race, a waste of time, a misguided act that gives the competition an advantage. The seventeenth-century philosopher Blaise Pascal was on to something when he said, "All the evil in the world can be traced to our inability to sit still in a room." Sheer nonsense or simple wisdom? It remains for many in our driven society that sitting still in their rooms would amount to madness or a kind of torture.

Gerald May's distinction holds for more than our approach to spirituality and prayer. How we search for a job, how we go about making friends or finding a lover, how we study, how we grow our gardens, how we take our vacations . . . will be fruitful to the extent that we go about these important activities willingly rather than willfully. When we stop trying too hard, what we're after often seems to come to us, or at least to meet us halfway. When psychologists write about "flow"—finding that inner rhythm that allows one to live spontaneously and function optimally—they are in sync with May's emphasis on "willing" as the healthier way to exercise will. And when athletes speak of being in a "zone"—where their exploits on the field or court appear effortlessly graceful—they are never trying too hard but trusting their ability and training. Experiencing the gracefulness of the "flow" or the effortlessness of the "zone" follows upon our readiness to approach the contests of life and all manner of things willingly rather than willfully. It holds for all performers and artists, and for the most ordinary of us.

Willful people, I've noticed, tend to get on our nerves. More often than not, they are concerned about their own goals over the common good. They are as offensive as most zealots and ideologues. They instinctively indulge in comparisons and see life as essentially competitive—and they are determined to be counted among the winners. Willing people like to win, but they aren't willing to win at all costs. They understand what is a game and what isn't—what really doesn't matter and what does. I think it's hard for willful individuals to pray. I suspect they use prayer as an edge, an advantage in the race for status, power, and the good life.

I THINK OF JESUS AS A MOST willing man. He never seemed to be in a hurry. There appears no schedule or itinerary that he had to follow. He invited people of all stripes to listen to him and to follow him if they wanted to. He certainly didn't sound like an American politician running for office. (It's a presidential election year as I write and the campaign ads are glaring examples of willfulness. I try to imagine a "willing" campaign without success.) Nor does it appear that Jesus ever insisted that what he was about to say was so important that one of the scribes or someone who could write should get it down. Rather he told stories or parables—a most willing way to teach. His commandment, if you could call it that, was to love God and your neighbor. As a storytelling rabbi, he remained mostly unflappable when his listeners didn't get his message. On the contrary, when people didn't understand his teaching about the kingdom of heaven or the dignity of the poor and powerless, Jesus appeared sad rather than angry. He wasn't going to force the good news on anybody.

I think Jesus' willingness was one of his most attractive features. And if Jesus is willing, dare we say God is willing? I do dare because I trust that even God, the mysterious and all powerful One, doesn't force his creation to bend to his saving will.

RECENTLY I READ A SUMMARY OF a short story by the Spanish writer Miguel Unamuno titled "Saint Manuel Bueno, Martyr." A young man returns to his home village to be with his dying mother. In the presence of the parish priest, the mother clutches her son's hand and begs him to pray for her. He does not answer his mother. As he and the priest leave her room he tells the priest that he could not pray for his mother because he does not believe in God. "That's nonsense," the priest says curtly. "You don't have to believe in God to pray."[18] This extraordinary reply underscores the distinction I emphasized between faith and belief in the first section of this journal. From time to time I talk to people who say they can't pray because they don't believe in God, meaning the God of theism, the superhuman God we project from our human, frail attempts to comprehend the mystery beyond our comprehension.

The God of theism is the God the writer Anne Lamott had in mind when she said there are two basic prayers: "Help me, Help me, Help me" and "Thank you, Thank you, Thank you." But this God is my God too. It's the only God most of us can imagine, and imagine we must. So, I smother my curiosity about the God beyond God and leave the "quest for the living God" to theologians and mystics. Like so many others, I've settled for a superparent God who is all loving, like the most loving people I've ever known, but raised to the millionth, millionth power. Don't be surprised that much of my prayer is the petition kind. I pray that God might heal friends, family, students who are seriously ill. I pray that I might be a good priest and make my Grandfather Cozzens proud. I pray for my wounded, divided, stumbling church that doesn't quite know what to make of the secular world in which it is embedded. I pray for the president of the United States, for his and his family's safety and that he might be a wise leader. I pray for world leaders that they might keep us from destroying ourselves. And I pray for justice—for the homeless and dispossessed, the abused and for the children who live in daily terror. This is only "right and just."

I understand that the God beyond God gets me closer to the holy, living God than does my superparent God. But I haven't quite learned at this point how to pray to this God. I'm satisfied to sit still in the presence of this

God. So my prayer to the God beyond God is wordless mostly. I'm quite sure my human attempts to imagine this God don't come close. I don't think this God is nice. Such a weak word. It appears G. K. Chesterton didn't think Christ was very "nice" when he wrote, "Christ is an extraordinary being with lips of thunder and acts of lurid decision, flinging down tables, casting out devils, passing with the wild secrecy of the wind from mountain isolation to a sort of dreadful demagogy." Rudolph Otto spoke of the God beyond God as compelling, fascinating mystery, drawing us like a magnet, and at the same time a terrifying mystery, prompting us to run like crazy from the awesome holiness of this great Other. If I don't think I would tremble before this God, I am a fool. And while I am gripped by a formless dread, at the same time I'm pulled toward this mystery, as though it were the only thing that mattered and my very life depended on drawing near.

We try, but we can't capture the God beyond God with our dogmas—as sacred as they may be. There is nothing like the experience of the numinous—and try as we might, we can't turn experience into dogma. If God is greater than religion, God is greater than dogma. Even an understanding of our hallowed doctrine of the Trinity isn't the final word. How can it be? We finite disciples and seekers will never have full or final comprehension of the infinite God; we will never speak or write the final word. That being the case, we nevertheless bravely continue as we must "our quest for the living God."

BECAUSE OF JESUS AND HIS Gospel I place my trust in this unknowable God. Because of Jesus I trust that the God beyond God is Goodness itself, a divine creative energy that is older than time—beyond time yet in time—and fresher than the next moment. And because of my Catholic roots, because of what I've experienced at Eucharist, I hold that this divinity is somehow, someway, relationality itself, communion itself.

> I pray to God to free me from God.
>
> — Meister Eckhart

ON MOST DAYS DURING THE academic year at the university where I teach, I have lunch with a half-dozen or so colleagues. Our conversations often turn to the painful issues of the contemporary Catholic Church and the divisive culture wars that seem to grow deeper and meaner by the day. Sometimes we talk about spirituality and prayer. Not surprisingly, when academics talk about prayer, the conversation tends to be brief—and a bit tense. For some of us, prayer is as necessary as the food we're eating for lunch. For others, prayer, especially prayer of petition, is pure superstition, a remnant of the medieval church ignorant of the world-changing rational and scientific breakthroughs of the Enlightenment.

Our infrequent conversations about prayer seldom go anywhere. We masters of dialogue and debate are strangely reticent here—I suspect out of respect for the unspoken religious or nonreligious positions represented at the table. Perhaps their reserve is a kind of deference to me as a priest. If begging prayer is little more than superstition, might not religion itself be superstition? And if that's the case, then their priest colleague has staked his life on a fallacy. If a few at the table think along these lines, they tread lightly here. But the question is fair. Aren't prayers of petition an attempt to change the mind of God? *"Well,"* God says, *"I was going to take your mother, but since you have prayed so hard, I will give her a few more years with you."* Do we, can we, change God's mind through our prayers?

Such scenarios are misleading, of course. For one thing, they suggest that God has a superhuman "mind" that oversees all of creation with unlimited discretionary powers that we mortals can influence if we but pray hard enough or long enough. Yet Jesus appears to have underwritten this understanding of prayer when he told his disciples that whatever they asked of God in his name would be granted to them. So I continue to pray for friends and family, for my stumbling church and for my wounded world. If this is superstition, I plead guilty. If this is self-contradictory, again I plead guilty. There is something at work here that I don't pretend to comprehend. I can live with that. Perhaps you've read the reports from particle physicists that subatomic particles can influence each other even though separated by enormous distances. Such reports lead me to imagine that creation is indeed in a state of unimaginable communion. The same reports, perhaps unreasonably, shore up my trust in prayers of petition and prayer itself.

Another troubling aspect of petitionary prayer is that it so easily reduces prayer to function. In other words, we can ask the all-American question: does it work? Over the years, dozens of students have written something like this in their reflection essays for my course in Christian Spirituality: "I've given up praying. I prayed so hard when my grandmother was suffering from her heart condition, but she still died." Their attitude seems to be, "If it works, fine. If it doesn't, I can't be bothered." Most can't see the subtle willfulness behind their prayers.

Perhaps we need to consider prayers of petition as a form of loving. When we pray for someone, we "want what is best" for them, we want what is truly good for them. As I noted earlier, Thomas Aquinas calls this love. Holding others in prayer is to hold them in love. And this, I believe, is one form of being in harmony with "the unseen order." It is "right and just" to pray for others as it is right and just to raise up prayers of praise and thanksgiving to God. Anne Lamott's "Thank you, Thank you,

Thank you" prayer arose spontaneously from the sheer relief of a tragedy avoided or a favor granted. When prayer is simply and fundamentally a spontaneous expression of humble gratitude for the fundamental gift of life and relationships, it comes close to pure prayer. And this prayer, too, is a form of loving.

MUCH OF WHAT I SEE OF gratitude today is reducible to good form, to rudimentary etiquette. I wonder how much of it is heartfelt. But sincere gratitude is at least an indirect form of prayer. If life itself is a gift—and for the person of faith, a gift from God—then our gestures of appreciation for human acts of kindness and thoughtfulness rise up from our faith-based impulse to acknowledge our finitude, our creaturehood.

A friend of mine described her very gifted and attractive high school daughter this way. "She's a wonderful young woman, smart, athletic, popular. She has one major flaw, though. She suffers from 'entitleitis.'" Later I heard that her daughter was cured of her affliction, her sense of entitlement, during a service trip to a Latin American country. "She came home," I was told, "a different young woman." When we understand that we are not little gods, that we are not the center of our world, something rings true in our souls. The monk-psychologist and spiritual writer, David Steindl-Rast, put it this way, "For happiness is not what makes us grateful. It is gratefulness that makes us happy." Ungrateful people are incapable of real happiness or peace of soul. They live in a restless world, blind to the serenity of soul we find when we live in harmony with the "unseen order." It's Steindl-Rast, by the way, who reminds us that we pray in order to lead prayerful lives. And prayerful living, silently but surely, draws us like a magnet to the unseen order.

> Prayer does not change
> God but it changes him who prays.

— Søren Kierkegaard

We swim, so to speak, in a sea of grace. And we are meant to be to grace like a fish is to water—moving rather smoothly, rather effortlessly, trusting that what we need to survive is already given. But we have this deeply engrained tendency—original sin?—not to trust this ocean of grace. We prefer to hold our breath. We close tight our gills. In this state, we dart about feverishly, aware of the silent pain we hold in our breasts, willfully seeking relief "in all the wrong places." It's prayer that opens our gills, often guardedly at first, and allows us to breathe in God's grace. And the more we trust that prayer isn't sheer foolishness or pious superstition, the wider we open our gills and allow the breath of the Spirit to sustain us. We learn to swim willingly rather than willfully. We sense the "unseen order" and allow the currents of grace to hold us in harmony with it.

The metaphor puts a different light on prayer. In this light, prayer is not so much what we do but who we are. We become prayer. Our very breathing in and breathing out is prayer. Our sitting down and standing up is prayer. Our doing dishes and taking out garbage is prayer. Our serious conversation is prayer. It's what Steindl-Rast meant when he wrote that we pray in order to lead prayerful lives. It's what St. Paul meant when he wrote that we should pray always. Therese of Lisieux wrote simply and beautifully about this reality and so did the French mystic Simone Weil. Weil stated without hedging that twenty minutes of concentrated study can purify the soul. We find the same insight in the spiritual classic *The Practice of the Presence of God*, a book drawn from the letters and kitchen talk of a seventeenth-century French Carmelite lay brother, Lawrence of the Resurrection, who was assigned to the monastery's scullery because he lacked a formal education. The heart of prayer for Brother Lawrence was to cultivate an awareness of the presence of God in his small world of pots and pans. This he believed, hallowed all the moments and activities of his day. In other words, conscious of the presence of God, we can move through our day in a "state of prayer."

Psychologists have a term for what Brother Lawrence understood as the core of his spirituality—*intentionality*. A story here is better than a definition. The story is set in Europe during the Middle Ages. On a hot and humid summer day, a merchant stands at the gate of a walled medieval city. Off in the distance, far down the road leading up to the city, he sees three peasant laborers, one behind the other, each pushing a wheelbarrow piled high with bricks. The merchant strides down the road toward the first man and holds up his hand signaling him to stop. "What are you doing?" he asks. The man puts the wheelbarrow down, squints at the merchant through narrow eyes, wipes the sweat from his brow, and answers curtly, "What does it look like I'm doing? I'm pushing a wheelbarrow full of bricks. It's as heavy as the day is hot." The merchant moves on to the second man and asks the same question. Grateful for even a brief rest, the peasant says, "I have a wife and children. If I don't work, they don't eat." The merchant thanks him and approaches the final worker and puts the very same question to him: "What are you doing?" This worker lowers his wheelbarrow and slowly straightens up. The merchant senses something different about this man. He's as sweaty and tired as the others, but after remaining silent for a few seconds, he says softly, "What am I doing?" His eyes brighten. "I'm building a cathedral."

Now the first worker was just working. If there was any "intentionality" here it was simply to make it through the day and then find some shade and something to drink. The second worker was working for his family. His "intentionality" was to provide for those he loved. His sense of purpose bestowed a certain dignity to his work, much like a single mother working into the night cleaning office buildings to put a child through school. Now the third workman also had a family and he too had to put food on the table. But he kept in mind that the bricks he was hauling into the city were to be used for the construction of a cathedral. This "intentionality" allowed him to work with a sense of humble pride and purpose. His labor was significant. Brother Lawrence would have said, I'm sure, that it was prayer.

(The construction of a medieval cathedral often took more than a hundred years. Many of those involved—patrons, architects, engineers, craftsmen, laborers—never saw their cathedral completed.)

At different times, I believe most of us feel like we are pushing brick-laden wheelbarrows in sweltering heat. Sometimes even the ordinary, daily routine and boredom of our lives seems unbearable. Understanding intentionality can be helpful here. The Gospel calls the baptized—from kitchen workers to chancery staffers—to build the Reign of God by following the Way of Christ. Prelates and laborers, educated and unlettered, haves and have-nots, we're part of a pilgrim people committed through baptism to building the kingdom. It's easy to forget that. Prayer allows us to focus our intentionality on what really matters, especially on what matters most.

So it's wise to assign times for prayer. No, I don't believe it is a sin to miss one's morning or night prayers. As I noted earlier in this journal, it's not a good idea for the church to motivate the faithful to do what is necessary and good for their spiritual lives by attaching the burden of "sin" to the failure to do what is understood as necessary and good. It may have "worked" in the past (I don't believe it ever really worked), but it certainly doesn't work today. Church authorities didn't seem to care if people were doing the right things for the wrong reasons. "Pray or else" was the message. "Pray, or else sin." Not only does it not work in the venial sin category—not saying one's morning prayers, for example— it doesn't work when it comes to mortal sin. Despite their religious upbringing, Catholics don't think they have sinned when they fail to say their morning prayers. And Catholics, it appears, don't think they have sinned mortally when they miss Sunday Mass. As central and theoretically essential as the Eucharist remains to the spiritual and faith life of Catholics, the dramatic drop in Mass attendance—on average about a quarter of the faithful celebrate Mass in the United States, and in the so-called Catholic countries of Europe, Sunday worship is in single digit percentages—is sending a clear message to church authorities: most Catholics who "miss Mass" don't go to bed Sunday night thinking they have committed mortal sin. These changes in private and public prayer deserve to be taken seriously. The Gospel and the rich spiritual heritage of the church make it clear that the simple wish to be a spiritual person living in harmony with the unseen order isn't sufficient. As Pascal discovered, we have to first learn to sit still and then we must pray, with words or in the silence of sitting in the presence of God. And our learning to sit still and pray requires some form of structure, some form of discipline.

Only then can we turn doing our dishes and pushing our wheelbarrows into prayer. It is prayerful living, living in the presence of God, that holds us in harmony with the unseen order. And this, indeed, is our "supreme good."

THE ENGLISH CARMELITE NUN, Wendy Beckett, believes prayer is the only human action or state where cheating is impossible. "As soon as pretense sets in, prayer stops." She's right of course, but on another level, we can imagine all sorts of cheating, all sorts of pretense. Sister Wendy knows it is dangerous to take the measure of anyone's prayer, even one's own. Nevertheless, I dare to venture into these dangerous waters. In my defense, I'm speaking of types or categories of prayer and not about the authenticity or worthiness of an individual's prayer. The sincerity and authenticity of another's prayer, and often one's own, is immeasurable. Still, cheating at prayer is possible.

St. Joseph Cupertino, the patron saint of students taking exams, gets a lot of attention from Catholic college students during finals week at the end of each semester. I remember praying to Joseph Cupertino as I studied for major exams during my seminary years. But if I hadn't been preparing for the exams, my prayers to this little-known saint—little known except in circles of panicky students too busy or lazy to study—would be in vain. I smile when people ask me, as a priest, to pray for nice weather for the parish picnic. I cringe when I hear people speak of praying before they head to a football game or to the casino. And I try to remain respectfully neutral when I'm asked about a certain novena or the nine first Fridays devotion. Perhaps this too can be a form of loving. I have my doubts.

Controlling behavior, I've noted, may be an indicator of below the surface willfulness. And blatantly controlling individuals, of course, wear their willfulness on their sleeves. Controlling prayer—prayer that tries to influence or control contingencies of various kinds, from "a nice day for the picnic" to global warming—is fundamentally willful prayer and often superstitious to its core. Sister Wendy Beckett puts it this way, "Controlled prayer is only partial prayer; it is the giving up the control to God that makes prayer true."

I MENTIONED EARLIER THAT IT'S a presidential election year as I write these pages. I can't imagine a U.S. politician acknowledging that he or she doesn't pray, especially a candidate for our highest office. So, prayer in our secular but strangely religious nation stands right up there with the civic virtue of voting and other forms of good citizenship. The point here is not the authenticity of a candidate's prayer but the unquestioned necessity to be perceived as a person of religious belief and prayer. From time to time, students will tell me of their families' practice of front-row Mass attendance every Sunday. "It's good for business," is how one daughter quoted her father, a local small business owner. Other students reported with a certain sadness that it was important for their parents not only to take the family to church every Sunday, but also to have their regular church attendance noticed. In some traditional circles, "respectable" people go to church on Sundays. But these circles are growing ever smaller. I like to think these shallow, superficial motivations for Sunday worship are minimal. More common, I believe, is a sense of religious obligation reinforced by the penalty of serious sin for skipping Mass. An older Catholic man put it this way, "I only go to Mass each Sunday to punch my 'stay out of hell card' for another week." Yet, as I've noted, this fear of hellfire is dying fast among Catholics of all generations.

WHILE "FEAR OF HELL" APPEARS to have worked for centuries in getting Catholics to church on Sunday, it is, for all practical purposes, dead in the water. And our bishops don't know what to do about it. Most are smart enough not to play the "mortal sin" card. They know it wouldn't work. Yet they remain reluctant to turn inward and measure the quality of Sunday Eucharist—from the homily to active participation, from a welcoming spirit to a true sense of community—and choose rather to blame the secular character of American society or the laxity and laziness of Catholic laity. The bishops would learn a great deal, I believe, from listening to the minority of Catholics who do celebrate Eucharist each week. Why don't they see Sunday Mass as an option they can simply pass up? Why can't they *not* go to Mass? I believe I know how they would answer.

They go to Mass because it's at the Lord's table that they sense most concretely the communion that's at the heart of Christianity. And from time to time, they keenly experience the divine presence in word and sacrament and in the assembly itself. They go to Mass to experience *holy communion*. In this holy communion they give thanks and pray for those in need and for those who suffer violence and injustice. While giving thanks they receive strength for the week ahead, for coping with the hardships in their lives. They would speak, however haltingly, of the correlation, or better, reciprocity, they see between their private prayers and the communal prayer of Eucharist. They would agree with Dorothy

Day's bold assertion: "I can put up with anything be-tween Eucharists." They find spiritual nourishment at Mass and thereby give us a clue to at least one of the causes of the falloff from weekly attendance—people who no longer go to Mass say they aren't nourished, spiritually nourished, from their public prayer.

I see little prayerful listening on the part of our bish-ops. Listening can be dangerous for church hierarchs. If they really listen to their people, they will be motivated to make changes or to take actions that are looked upon with suspicion by the Vatican power structure. So, many bishops listen only for the directives that come from Rome. Frustrated and cowed, they wring their hands and hope for the best. More managers than leaders, they remain busy fretting over finances and, in most of our larger dioceses, closing churches.

What the Mystics Know

PRAYER, THE MYSTICS TELL US, makes us real. We might ask, "What's that supposed to mean?" Since the time of Descartes, if we're thinking, we're real. If we don't pray, does that make us unreal? The mystics would answer, yes; at least we're not as real as we might be. How can that be?

I'm thinking about my friend, Sister Kilian Huf-gard, an Ursuline nun of Cleveland, a daring artist—she once painted an icon in oil rather than the required egg tempera—a professor of the philosophy and history of art, and a scholar who devoted her academic life to the study of St. Bernard of Clairvaux's theory of art and architecture. Almost a generation older than I, Sister Kilian agreed to tutor me on the history and theory of art in her Ursuline College studio on Thursday afternoons. She was perhaps the most interesting and fascinating woman I've ever known. I say that because she was likely the most real person I've ever known. Sister Kilian spoke softly, and at first I took that to reflect a certain tentativeness of spirit. I was quite wrong here. She proved to be one of the most passionate, articulate of scholars when she spoke of art and its inherent relationship to all that is real. But I don't want to get ahead of my story.

Kilian Hufgard demonstrated a freedom of soul, an authenticity of spirit, and a soothing "at homeness" that unfailingly put me at ease in her company. Ease isn't quite the right word. I was at peace in her company. On those Thursday afternoons, I felt I was in the presence of a woman who had learned to live in harmony with God's unseen order.

What follows here is Hufgard's path to the unseen order. Her fundamental touchstone for reality and for art was her concept of the good, not the beautiful, but the good. She agreed with Mircea Eliade who believed that "spirituality is strange, it has an obligation to create."

Created in the image of God the creator, men and women indeed had an obligation to create, that is, to be makers and artists. Hufgard rejected the distinction between the fine arts and crafts and proposed that art is better understood as the general term embracing all human skill— all creativity. Art, for her, was the making well of that which needs to be made with skill and knowledge. And when something is made with skill and knowledge that serves the human spirit and human needs, it is thereby *good*. And for Sister Kilian and the mystics, that which is good is that which is truly real.

It was easy for Sister Kilian and me to apply these lessons to the art of living. She smiled in agreement when I quoted from Cicero's *De Amicitia,* "Nothing is more lovable than goodness" (*Nihil enim virtute amabilius*). A good person—however handsome or plain—understood in this light, is always attractive. And conversely, the most physically beautiful people, if not good, soon wear thin on those around them. Surface beauty without inner goodness, we concluded, was inevitably boring or worse, intolerable. From the mystic's perspective, whatever isn't good, whatever isn't authentic and true, isn't real. Sister Kilian helped me to see how much of our cities and homes are cluttered with things plastic and artificial, unnecessary things displayed to impress. All this, of course, isn't good for the soul.

I write now from my apartment in Shaker Heights, a Cleveland suburb named for the religious sect of Shakers famous for their simplicity of life and for making things, especially furniture, with skill and mindfulness. The Shakers came close to embodying Kilian Hufgard's theory of art and architecture. A Shaker chair, for example, rings true with goodness, with the quality we associate with something made well and by hand and with purpose. A Shaker chair is real. So were the abbey churches emphasizing light, space, and line designed in accord with Bernard of Clairvaux's theory of architecture. The off-white colors, the focus on function, the scale of line and dimension all spoke to the simplicity—and reality—of monastic life. Bernard's minimalist spirit created and sustained for his monks an atmosphere of prayerful transcendence.

Contemporary mystics like Sister Wendy Beckett and Sister Kilian Hufgard stand in line with the medieval mystics who understood the link between prayer and being real. "Making us real is the effect of prayer, just as it is its accompaniment," writes Sister Wendy. Unless it's cheating prayer, superstitious or artificial prayer, prayer frees us from all that is unreal, all that is artificial and phony in life. And the mystics know that we are free only to the extent that we are real. We are capable of loving only to the extent that we are real. Anything real is by definition good. There are signs that even our popular culture may get this. A high compliment today may sound something like, "Man, that was so real!" "It was real!" signals a high tribute for something we find truly good.

> In humility is perfect freedom.

> — Thomas Merton

MY STUDENTS AT JOHN CARROLL UNIVERSITY are quick to get the distinction Thomas Merton makes between the false self and the true self. Perhaps it's because they are equally quick to spot the difference between students who are "posed" rather than "poised." Not surprisingly, they disdain whatever, whoever, they judge to be phony. Merton gives them both a theological vocabulary and an anthropology to assist them in their struggle to be real.

For Merton, the false self (I prefer "ego-self" because it's less judgmental.) is the self we present to the world. It's the self that wants to know how it's doing. It's the self that measures and compares his or her accomplishments with the accomplishments of others. It's the self that is always competing, secretly or openly, to come in first. I'm sympathetic to the false self. Our modern culture's emphasis on image, on fashion, on the material signs of status and success reinforce at every turn the pseudoreality of the false self. But the false self only deepens our anxieties, our fears, and insecurities. The false self tells us we will be more real if we only had more stuff, if we could only move in the right crowd, if we could only travel to the right locations and dine in the right restaurants and dance in the right clubs. For most people, the false self never quite measures up. So it tries harder, works longer hours, plunges more deeply into the race, strives ever more relentlessly to be in control. To the false self, the suggestion to sit still in a room, to possibly pray, just doesn't compute. The false self can't help but to be willful and restless.

Merton confessed he knew a great deal about the false self. It was his basic, almost full-time self until he got sick of being spiritually sick and found the path that led to the Catholic Church where, without struggle and with a convert's fervor, he sank ever so willingly into the deep well of monastic, mystical spirituality. At Gethsemani, now delivered and liberated from the discordant rhythms and chaotic energy of smoke-filled Manhattan jazz clubs, he discovered, for the first time in his life, true freedom of soul. In the solitude and silence of the Cistercian enclosure, Thomas Merton discovered his true self.

It is rather superficial but still accurate to say that Merton's understanding of the true self is the antithesis of the false self. Where the false self is willful, the true self is willing. Where the false self strives for mastery, the true self trusts the Gospel admonition not to worry and instead to live in "harmony." Where the false self compares and competes, the true self is at home in its own skin. Where the false self is self-conscious, the true self is poised but not posed, radiating the calm of just being included in God's communion of saints. While the false self cares very much what others think of it, the true self hardly bothers about the opinions of others. While the false self is quick to judge the motivations of others, the true self refuses the impossible task of judging the motives behind alienating and destructive behaviors. Where the false self is boastful, the true self is humble. Where the false self takes offense, the true self remains at peace.

But we must go deeper. The false self's identity is reinforced in the public square. The true self's identity is hidden in God. Like St. Augustine, the mystics understand that our deepest desire, whether recognized or not, is to experience communion with the divine. Merton's true self senses the divine spark embedded in the depths of its self—and at the same time, suspects it is embedded in the divine. "You will know that I am in my Father, and you in me, and I in you" (John 14:20).

> In order to become myself I must cease
> to be what I always thought I wanted to be,
> and in order to find myself I must go out of
> myself, and in order to live I have to die.

— Thomas Merton

IT WOULD BE A MISTAKE TO think that we live either in our false self or our true self. Except for the saints in our midst (and even here I have my doubts), we move more or less regularly from our true self to our false self and back again to our true self. It's part of the rhythm of the spiritual life. But prayer holds our feet to the fire. Prayer, especially the silent prayer of sitting in the presence of God, allows us to intuit (it's more intuition than anything else) how to live our ordinary lives more in our true selves than our false selves. In prayer we stumble upon the intuition that draws us into harmony with the unseen order. In prayer we learn to surrender, in the sense of trust, to the God beyond God. In prayer we catch glimpses of the innate communion holding creation—in all of its mystery, power, and beauty—in the hand of God.

And in prayer, the mystics remind us, we learn how to be real. Without the discipline of prayer, we can't help but remain somewhat inauthentic, somewhat unreal. Without the discipline of prayer, we live out our lives in the unreality of the false self. In Merton's words,

> People who know nothing of God and whose lives are centered on themselves, imagine that they can only find themselves by asserting their own desires and ambitions and appetites in a struggle with the rest of the world. They try to become real by imposing themselves on other people, by appropriating for themselves some share of the limited supply of created goods and

thus emphasizing the difference between themselves and other men who have less than they, or
nothing at all.

They can only conceive one way of becoming real: cutting themselves off from other
people and building a barrier of contrast and
distinction between themselves and other men.[19]

(I MET THOMAS MERTON AT Gethsemani in the summer
of 1967 thanks to a Carmelite nun who contacted one
of Merton's literary secretaries on my behalf. At the time
of our meeting, I was unaware of his spirit-shaking affair with "Margie," the nurse he met while hospitalized
in Louisville for back surgery. Perhaps it was Merton's
own lingering turmoil of soul that left me unmoved by
our meeting.)

INTERESTINGLY, THE MORE WE become people of prayer,
the more enchanting our world becomes. I should be
careful here. I'm thinking of how the term "enchantment" falls on the ears of women and men under the yoke
of rank injustice, brutal violence, and spirit-quenching
squalor. At the same time, there can be more enchantment in the hovels of the poor and exploited than in our
affluent suburbs. Moreover, the term is easily dismissed
today as in the past. Enlightenment rationalists had
little patience for the "enchanted" medieval world—a
world of spirits, demons, and moral forces. It conjured

up images of magic forests and skittish fairies. I have something else in mind. I'm thinking of Jesus' teaching that the "Kingdom of God is within." I'm thinking of what happens to our inner world when we learn to live in harmony with the unseen order. I'm thinking of the awakening that follows upon living in the presence of God. Enchantment for me captures the state of wonder and awe that comes over most of us from time to time that takes us "out of time," what I wrote about earlier in this journal as an ecstatic experience of transcendence. When our prayer puts us in touch with reality's enchanted character, we break through the crust of all that is superficial and boring and find an unexpected peace and an inexplicable joy.

I tell my students that an enchanted interior life is like being in love in the romantic sense of the term. When in love, everything remains the same, yet everything is different. It's what Merton meant when he called us all to surrender our awful solemnity and join in the "cosmic dance." Most of us, it seems to me, aren't in love most of the time. But we can be in love with life itself, with the mystery of it all and the promise of it all. On our own, without prayer and the openness it prompts to the sea of grace all about us, we live two-dimensional lives that inevitably turn inauthentic and boring. It's then that we do stupid things to escape our terrible tedium. Here the false self rules. So prayer makes us real and takes us into the realm of enchantment. Here the true self breathes in the air of freedom and "reality."

In our secular age, the cards seem stacked against the enchanted life—the meaningful life, the life of gratitude and praise, of wonder and awe. There's simply too much violence, too much injustice, too much greed to speak of enchantment. For many today these hard forces of reality have destroyed religion's credibility and exposed its false hope. There's only the "real" world where we work a lot, suffer much, love a little, grow old and die, often alone. Here all "realistic" thinking people see no possibility of enchantment, of "higher meanings" lurking behind the grandeur of our universe.

No matter the cards we've been dealt, no matter the hard realities of our lives, the mystics insist on the possibility of enchantment, understood as the graced sense of the presence of the divine. When we move from our false self into the glow of our true self—*enchantment*. When we try to understand without judgment the meanness we see in others, when we forgive or experience forgiveness—*enchantment*. When compassion moves us to action, when family meals heal hurts and tensions—*enchantment*. When lovers really love, when children learn to share, when we silently grieve those who have died—these and other common experiences hold the potential for spiritual delight. Glorious sunsets, silent stars on cloudless nights, beams of gold sunlight breaking through tall trees—all these are "rumors of angels," hints of our enchanted world.

IT SHOULDN'T SURPRISE THAT IT'S the monks and nuns of our past and present that have the most to say about life's enchanted character. Nor should it surprise us that their lives are built around and on the pillars of prayer. True, monasticism has its own struggles today. And we see vowed religious women ministering outside monastic enclosures coping—creatively and bravely—with mostly empty novitiates and average ages that climb ever higher into the late seventies. But if I'm right, the monks and nuns know the most about what it takes to lead an enchanted life. They know more than we priests do. Our average age is sixty-five—I think of us as the church's Medicare Corps—and we older priests protest we are too tired and discouraged to be enchanted. Our younger brothers, however, have found a certain enchantment in their turn to baroque vestments, high liturgies, and their stable and secure world of hierarchy, dogmatic certainties, and canonical order. But their effete clerical world reeks to me of unreality. There are lay mystics, of course, who write persuasively about enchantment and the mystery of grace. Dorothy Day and Simone Weil come to mind, but most don't have the platform enjoyed by monks and nuns for the secular media to pay much attention.

MORRIS BERMAN, AUTHOR OF *The Twilight of American Culture* (and previously the author of *The Reenchantment of*

the World) argues that holding on to the best of our culture is fundamentally a matter of individual conscience
and the rise of what he calls a new "monastic individual."
Berman certainly isn't calling for thinking individuals
sensitive to the inauthenticity and corruption in modern
society to leave their families and jobs and drive off to
the nearest monastery. But he is calling for thinking individuals to learn from the enchanted world of monks and
nuns. He's calling for men and women to live outside
monastic walls with the mindfulness and intentionality
of monks and nuns. Only such individuals will be as-
tute enough to see the decay and disenchantment of our
Western civilization. As I read Berman, he's calling for
enough individuals to embrace a "secular spirituality,"
enough to reach a tipping point that would turn our
modern culture around and away from what he sees as
certain decline. His "new monks and nuns" would be
able to sit still in a room, to work for the common good,
and would prize that which is real and good over the
adolescent titillations and dark violence of modern film
and music.

To a great extent, Merton would agree with Berman.
If we are to avoid destroying our world and ourselves,
we might begin by robing ourselves in the conscience
and discipline of the monk and nun. Merton, certainly,
understood that the real world vibrates with rhythms of
enchantment where goodness trumps the banal, where

wisdom trumps technology, and compassion trumps power. Preserving this enchanted dimension for our fragmented culture may well rest in the hands of Berman's "new monastic individuals," in the hands of the poor and powerless, in the hands of those free enough to sense the unseen order that holds us in holy communion.

WHERE DO WE LEARN TO TRUST that God is good, that Jesus is the Christ, that the Holy Spirit breathes into our lungs the healing communion of grace? Where, for that matter, do we learn to pray? To ask "where" is perhaps misleading since it implies a place. The answer, while it implies place, transcends place without denying its grounding necessity. We learn to trust, to love, to believe, to hope in what we might call the nonact of sitting still—or, better, in the perfectly pure act of sitting still. Pascal understood this. So do the mystics and saints of our own day. Almost every aspect of our interior lives depends on or is influenced by the quality of our stillness.

> We have to earn silence . . . to work for it:
> to make it not an absence but a presence;
> not emptiness but repletion. Silence is something
> more than just a pause; it is that enchanted
> place where space is cleared and time is
> stayed and the horizon itself expands.
>
> — Pico Iyer

I LEARNED SOMETHING ABOUT stillness during my eight years of seminary. During my pre–Vatican II seminary training, my classmates and I lived basically monastic lives that hardly differed from that of monks in their enclosures. The "grand silence," a rigidly imposed rule of complete silence from compline, our common night prayer, to grace before breakfast, set the tone of seminary stillness. Daily meditation, spiritual reading, silent walks to pray the rosary, and our long hours of study taught us seminarians how to make peace with stillness. And more than make peace with stillness, to actually treasure it as the very ground of our spiritual lives. (I've recognized for many years the shortcomings of my seminary education and formation—theology textbooks in Latin, unbalanced spiritual formation, disregard for the principles of psychological health and maturity, a negative emphasis on human sexuality, among others. My theological education proved to be little more than medieval apologetics. I was never encouraged to think creatively or critically—or even pastorally, for that matter.) So, when I'm asked today about my seminary years, I unfailingly say I remember gratefully that my "monastic" formation instilled in me an enduring regard for the central place of stillness and silence in my interior life. It was during my seminary years that I learned the difference between loneliness and aloneness, between isolation and solitude. And later, as a priest and spiri-

tual director, I learned to respect the need for balancing
solitude and ministry, the holy rhythm of sitting still and
moving out to others and sitting still again before moving out again.

> Solitude is such a potential thing. We hear
> voices in solitude, we never hear in the
> hurry and turmoil of life; we receive
> counsels and comforts, we get under
> no other condition.

— Amelia Edith Huddleston Barr

A GOOD PART OF THE MONASTIC genius is its profound
regard for the place of solitude in the life of monks and
nuns. And in recent years, monastic writers like Thomas
Merton and Thomas Keating see solitude as important,
even essential, for the spiritual lives of us all, layperson,
monk or nun, bishop or pope. This holds true no matter
where our personalities and temperaments fall on the
extrovert-introvert continuum.

Still, solitude can be terrifying. For many, it's just
another name for loneliness—the black hole we know
as the restless, painful ache in the hollow of our personal core. Existentialist writers like Camus and Sartre understand the breadth of this human ache and its
inescapable rootedness in the human condition. Moral courage, they propose, in the vein of Paul Tillich's
"courage to be," is our only path through this grey

cloud of alienation and abandonment. Other paths, the paths of denial, distraction, power, and greed, ultimately take us deeper into the blackness. So, yes, solitude can be terrifying. Like a spiritual virus, solitude, so the thinking goes, breeds loneliness. Moreover, prisoners say solitary confinement is the worst of all forms of punishment. It's no surprise then that solitude makes little sense in our secular, disenchanted world, unless its aim is to give permission to briefly step out of the race in order to rest up a bit only to better rejoin the race for success and fortune.

IT'S TRUE THAT SOLITUDE HAS its dangers. Some individuals who compulsively pursue solitude have troubled personalities. Others are paralyzed by the mere thought of intimacy or even ordinary forms of social interaction. But these disturbed souls are in the minority. Many relatively healthy individuals—hardly the neurotic type—can't tolerate being alone without turning on the radio or television or their personal computers. I hear there are homes with TV's in every room, including the bathroom. Without some form of distraction, physical aloneness leaves large numbers of us edgy and restless. For some, their work, their hobbies, their driven efforts to fill their free time with all kinds of busyness, are flights from solitude. We can't take a walk around the block without our cell phone. We can't sit on a bus without texting or tweeting. Yet, in our disenchanted world, many of our social engagements and pursuits of entertainment leave us feeling alienated or estranged—from what, we aren't sure. And the more superficial our society becomes, the more narrowly secular it becomes, the more likely we are to return to our homes and households feeling edgy and restless.

YET, THE POINT I'M TRYING TO make here, that real prayer and real transformation in Christ are grounded in solitude and stillness remains fuzzy. Hermann Hesse, in these few lines, comes closer than most.

> We must become so alone, so utterly alone, that we withdraw into our innermost self. It is a way of bitter suffering. But then our solitude is overcome, we are no longer alone, for we find that our innermost self is the spirit, that it is God, the indivisible. And suddenly we find ourselves in the midst of the world, yet undisturbed by its multiplicity, for [in] our innermost soul, we know ourselves to be one with all being.

HESSE LINKS HERE WHAT I'VE been trying to say so far in this journal: that trust and communion, that faith, hope, and love, grow out of our ability to sit still in a room, to sit through the anguish of our loneliness and our grieving until it gives birth to a new and unexpected holy communion. Instead, at least some of the time, we run

from our loneliness and move with pseudobravery into
the abyss of our shallow and superficial world.

WHILE I'VE INDEED LEARNED much about stillness and
solitude from my seminary years with its bedrock life of
prayer, I've had my doubts along the way. Might solitude be an illusion or simply an escape from reality?
Might the wordless prayer it spawned be mere fantasy?
Would a serious, disciplined prayer life allow me to live
a full and healthy life as a celibate priest? Merton, the
master chronicler in our day of solitude's place in the life
of prayer and interior transformation, seemed to gamble
away his persuasive and elegant writings about the har-
monies of the solitary life when he wrote with stunning
candor about his love for Margie, a nurse he met while
recovering from surgery in 1966.[20] I have the utmost
sympathy for Merton. I've been in his shoes. Can true
contemplatives and celibates like Merton fall in love?
Oh yes, yes they can. And I don't believe this profoundly human experience negates in the least their need for
solitude and stillness. I say this because, while I've never
completely lost my thirst for solitude and stillness, I've
come to love deeply, love deeply as a celibate priest. And,
as I suspected, loving deeply has strengthened my commitment to the Gospel and to ministry. My seminary
professors would roundly disagree.

I say this with the understanding that celibacy is
most likely my truth. I feel I have *grown into it* over

the past half century. The few times I've fallen in love have rocked my spiritual boat. But I never doubted, down deep, my truth as a priest. Nor did I ever experience a compelling drive to leave the priesthood and marry. Was I afraid? I don't know. I often thought of Edward Schillebeeckx's insight that celibacy for those who have the charism manifests itself as "an inability to do otherwise." Now as a senior celibate, I believe I know something about loneliness. It can be an agreeable companion. It greets me every evening when I return home from the university. It's with me every weekend. I believe it has helped me to look with understanding and empathy on those who live alone—the elderly and unmarried, widows and widowers, the divorced and separated. I know that loneliness remains, if not at the center, then close to the center of the human condition, *pace* Camus and Sartre.

So, when my brother Jim called at four in the afternoon, as he often did before his too-early death, to invite me over for orange roughy and white wine, I smiled in anticipation. When my brother Tom calls on a Sunday afternoon to invite me for dinner, I drop what I'm doing. When my sister Maryellen invites me to supper on her patio, I can hardly wait. I should be used to it by now, but I don't like eating alone. And often enough, after eating out, I'm happy to return home for a late evening of *The Anonymous 4* and the consoling solitude of vespers, the evening prayer of the church, the evening prayer of the priest.

> Being solitary is being alone well:
> being alone luxuriously immersed in doing
> things of your own choice, aware of the
> fullness of your own presence rather than
> of the absence of others. Because solitude
> is an achievement.
>
> — Alice Koller

ONE OF MY SEMINARY SPIRITUAL directors surprised me when he said that spiritual reading was *almost* more important for the spiritual life than prayer. He believed strongly that good spiritual reading nourished and sustained prayer and that without it, our prayer lives would flounder. He was right. He could have added that prayer, in turn, whets our appetite for spiritual reading.

MY FORTY FIRST-YEAR SEMINARY CLASSMATES and I slept in two large dormitory rooms with lockers next to our beds for our cassocks, pants, underwear, and things. Our textbooks and spiritual reading materials were stored in our study-hall desks on the floor below. There was no reading in bed. The lights were turned off at 10 pm, and the electricity was cut, save for the jakes (seminary slang for the bathrooms). Had I been able to read into the night, it would have been Thomas Merton's classic *The*

Seven Storey Mountain. It's hard to exaggerate the influence this book had on my spiritual life and my desire to be a priest. My "first-fervor" coupled with my reading of *The Seven Storey Mountain* made me the perfect seminarian—devout, docile, athletic, agreeable. By the time I moved to the major seminary and my final years of study for the priesthood, there was a clear contemplative character to my spirituality due no doubt to my temperament but strengthened and deepened by my correspondence with Sister Colette of the Trinity, a young nun in the Carmelite Monastery in Baltimore, who now, fifty years later, is the prioress there. Her letters, written in measured script that could only have flowed from stillness and silence, were in themselves spiritual reading. She, like Merton at Gethsemani, was caught up in the first-fervor of her new enchanted world as a cloistered nun and wrote with the unselfconscious idealism of one who was falling in love with God.

LESS THAN TWO YEARS AWAY FROM ordination, I sat before my priest spiritual director and acknowledged I was just then pulling out of a major spiritual drought that had raised all kinds of disturbing questions, questions swirling around the rightness of proceeding on to ordination. He wanted to know how I made it through this difficult time. Perhaps he wondered why I hadn't come to speak to him earlier. I surprised him when I explained that good spiritual reading had been the turning point. I called it "biblio-therapy." He was speechless.

Though I more often dipped rather than plunged into the Carmelite spiritual masters—Teresa of Avila, John of the Cross, Therese of Lisieux—they have left their mark. I believe it's no accident that much of my seminary spiritual reading came from the pens of contemplative writers. More recently, I've been nourished by Romano Guardini, Jean Sulivan, Henri Nouwen, Dorothy Day, John O'Donohue, Kathleen Norris, and Richard Rohr. I cast a pretty wide net when it comes to spiritual reading. Works of theology are included here, as well as church history, especially the recent gems from James Carroll (*Constantine's Sword, Practicing Catholic, Jerusalem, Jerusalem*); some fiction (and not only the works of the so-called Catholic novelists); and the poetry of Seamus Heaney, Wendell Berry, and Mary Oliver. All that we call "good literature" fits nicely in my net. These named and unnamed writers of "good literature" awakened my spirit, caught me up with the alertness one feels when encountering something true and good and real. Reading such authors, I found that I regularly had to pause and reflect. And yes, pray. Our Catholic tradition has a name for that kind of reading—*lectio divina.* Good spiritual reading—the Scriptures hold a preeminent place here—unfailingly slows us down to a point of energizing stillness. Always a sign of grace.

WITHOUT SOUND SPIRITUAL READING our interior lives tend to draw us down different paths—all potentially misleading. We tend to reduce the spiritual life to ethical living, to "saying" our prayers, and to holding fast to church dogmas. Or we tend to become pious in the sense that our spirituality takes on a sentimental character where the comforts of belief hold sway. Without sound spiritual reading, religion and the spiritual life become a kind of "eternal life insurance policy." Left on their own without the guidance of spiritual reading, religious individuals often become rigidly judgmental and even extremist as they see their cherished certainties challenged by a nonbelieving, ever more secular populace.

Spiritual reading, my spiritual director understood, holds a key place in the struggle of contemporary seekers to remain spiritually alive in our fast-paced and secular world where for many it is a sin to slow down. But if we do slow down and our hearts are right, the books we need seem to find us. If we are more or less in harmony with the unseen order, we need but to be patient and alert.

Contemplative Living

MUCH OF CONTEMPORARY LIFE IN the West seems out of balance or out of sync. In the previous pages I've tried to highlight symptoms of this imbalance. It seems to me we are becoming ever more neurotic, anxious, and fearful. Today the mostly dismissed existentialist philosophers of the twentieth century are making tepid signs of resurgence. Make the best of it, they say. Get as much out of life as you can by being as authentic as you can and as brave as you can. That's it really. But what if the atheist existentialists are right? What if life is meaningless, even absurd? What if Nietzsche was right? My earlier entries on faith and communion fall lifeless to the floor. There is, then, no intimacy or transcendence, no veiled sphere of enchantment, no self-giving love, no heroism, no greatness of soul, no unseen order save that of power. Added to this bleak perspective, our houses of worship, already shrines for the devout, become museums to our capacity to be duped by the lies of religion. So we no longer build churches but sprawling shopping malls, vast stadiums for the worship of our hero athletes and rock stars, and megatheaters to help us escape from our spiritual despair in pornographic violence and mayhem.

They exaggerate, you say. Whether they do or not isn't the point. The point is that we are in real moral danger—and physical danger. In the midst of goodness all about, there are growing strains of darkness and evil. Hasn't it ever been so? Yes, but that too isn't the point. The point is to see the critical need for a growing critical mass of global villagers who live so rightly and act so responsibly that human misery and exploitation are diminished rather than increased. The point is to make the mass truly critical. For the critical mass is the Reign of God in history. Carl Jung said simply and directly, "If you want peace, be a peaceful person." Jung understood the network of our fundamental human communion as the "collective unconscious." An individual person, living peacefully anywhere in the world contributes to the peace of the world. I believe Jung was on to something. By extension, if you want justice, be a just person. And if this be so, by taking one's spiritual life seriously, an individual contributes to the critical mass that we Christians call the Reign of God. And this critical mass, in turn, leads to the kind of political, diplomatic, and social action that fosters peace and justice in our time.

So, I don't believe it's a cop-out to earnestly try to be a peaceful person, a just person in the face of the world's staggering injustice and disordering chaos. Right action will flow from such centered people. And wrong action will be minimized. And where no action is visible, the collective unconscious is still at work cultivating the soil of our collective soul.

I SHOULD SAY SOMETHING HERE about the difference between "living in the presence of God" and "contemplative living." Both emphasize the importance of mindfulness and awareness, of living in the "now." Both respect the significance of intentionality's role in the search for a meaningful life. And both urge us to slow down and appreciate the dignity and grace of the ordinary, the "taken for granted" aspects of everyday life.

While "living in the presence of God" assumes a belief in God, or a trusting faith in the God beyond God, "contemplative living" has a broader horizon. There are men and women today leading contemplative lives who don't believe in God. Some self-identify as agnostic. These include many of the "I'm spiritual but not religious" population who at the same time show interest in the God beyond the God they hear of. They lead rich, reflective, meditative lives nourished by good literature and the fine and performing arts. They give evidence of concern for the common good and are generous with their time and money for worthy causes. They instinctively understand their need to sit still from time to time. I believe they sense there might indeed be an unseen order and that they should try to live in harmony with it. But "living in the presence of God" is something they would never claim.

The two modes of living look very much like the other and *are* very much like the other. The distinction, however, should be maintained. In summary, living in the presence of God is always contemplative living. Contemplative living, on the other hand, is not necessarily living in the presence of God.

I'VE WRITTEN AT SOME LENGTH about the silent, wordless, often imageless, prayer called contemplative or centering prayer. Now, from a different perspective, this "sitting in the presence of God prayer" has a purifying power that allows us to see instinctively what really matters, what matters most. "Be still," the psalmist says, "and know that I am God." Be still, in other words, and know that you are not God. Be still and have faith, be still and hope, be still and love. Our stillness, metaphorically speaking, breaks down the walls of our monasteries and lets the contemplative charism escape into the streets of our global village where it's "infecting" ever growing numbers.

People tired of being out of balance, out of sync, tired of being spiritually sick are experimenting with contemplative prayer and reporting extraordinary, if subtle, changes in their lives. They say they are more centered and less restless; they tend not to judge others, they seem more content with what they have; they are more patient with spouses, children, and co-workers. They report being less neurotic, less anxious, less fearful. In a word—they are peaceful. Jung is smiling.

Contemplative prayer, as we have seen, sooner than later leads to contemplative living. And contemplative living makes a defining difference in our broken world. By contemplative living I'm referring, with repeated urgency, to the quality of awareness, of mindfulness, that prompts us to live fully in the present moment. Contemplative living honors the now. It is instinctively willing rather than willful. And because those who live contemplative lives force nothing, they move gracefully through their day. When held up in traffic or waiting in line, these secular contemplatives often turn to silent prayer. Little things don't upset them. If this sounds idealistic and unreal, I believe there are people in each of our lives that are living precisely this way. Try to spot them.

SIGNS OF CONTEMPLATIVE PRAYER'S steady if slow emergence in our parishes and beyond are easy enough to find. Parish bulletins announce the meetings of contemplative prayer groups and offer invitations to "quiet" retreat days. Merton's books on contemplative prayer continue to sell. College courses on Christian spirituality feature the writings of contemplative writers and offer "lab" experiences of contemplative prayer. My own students are eager to read Dorothy Day's work and marvel at the contemplative spirituality embedded in her social activism and the Catholic Worker movement. Some students, put off by "religion's hypocrisy," are nevertheless drawn to what they sense as the authenticity and puzzling simplicity of contemplative prayer.

Beyond Catholic parishes and campuses, growing numbers of professionals carve contemplative prayer time out of their work day or lunch time. Vague reports like these may be meaningless and unfounded, but they inspire hope in me. I've heard rumors of contemplative prayer meetings for members of Congress and their staffs. (I assume these prayer groups represent rather evenly both political parties.) Meeting for contemplative prayer allows individuals from different political (and religious) traditions to meet on common ground where concern for the common good is reinforced. Moreover, true contemplatives are open-minded, able to see issues and situations from another's perspective. They have a keen eye that allows them to see through to the bulwarked, inflexible core of ideologies. They listen differently in this sense—they listen not only to be informed, but to be transformed. And they speak differently—having found their voice, there is no need for pseudo-elegance or shrill bombastic.

With all my energy, I hope and trust that the critical mass grows. Margaret Mead reminds us that relatively small and seemingly insignificant numbers of people have made great changes throughout history. Perhaps we're closer to the tipping point than we might think. Learning to live contemplatively is critical not only for our personal well-being, but I trust it is obvious, for the well-being of our global village and the earth itself.

A FEW RANDOM FINAL THOUGHTS. . . . Somehow, people who meet regularly for contemplative prayer discover the bonding effect of faithful sitting in the presence of God. I wonder what would happen if White House staff meetings and sessions of Congress and congressional committee meetings began with even a few minutes of silence. Sitting still is good—even for agnostics and the skeptical. Before I do anything that requires tact—a phone call, a brief note or card, an e-mail, a face to face meeting—I try to sit still for a minute or so. This brief moment of solitude tends to center me. I believe I speak or write more thoughtfully and in the case of meetings, I listen more openly and less defensively. Sitting still raises our consciousness like nothing else. In the silence we discover that it is not only what is said that matters, but when it is said and how it is said.

CONTEMPLATIVE PRAYER, WHILE NOT the only path to contemplative living, remains the truest path, at least from my experience. I sometimes think our only hope rests in an ever-expanding arc of men and women, from all corners of our planet, living contemplatively. More than through diplomacy, government intervention, military power, or economic policy, the violence and injustice of our world will be diminished by men and women leading contemplative lives. Put less starkly, only a contemplative factor in diplomacy, politics, and economics will prove ultimately effective.

I'LL CONCLUDE THIS SECTION WITH striking words from two of the twentieth century's major theologians. Turning to the level of the individual, Raimon Panikkar writes, "In this crucible of the modern world, only the mystic (contemplative) will survive. All others are going to disintegrate; they will be unable to resist either the physical strictures or the psychical strains." And from Karl Rahner, "The Christian of the twenty-first century will be a mystic (contemplative) or not at all."

POWER

I'VE KNOWN, IN A MODEST enough manner, the taste of power. As vicar for clergy in a large U.S. diocese, I enjoyed what politicos call access—access to power. It was, overall, a new and potentially seductive experience. Some of my brother priests looked at me with regard. Access to power, I discovered, was itself power. Each Monday morning at 8:30 I met with my bishop to review issues, concerns, and problems relating to the five hundred or so priests in the diocese of Cleveland. Most of these meetings dealt with rather mundane concerns— the appointments of pastors, changes in priestly assignments, hospitalized priests, parishioners' complaints of bullying or insensitive pastors, priests with personal problems such as alcohol abuse or "inappropriate relationships" with women. (We dealt with allegations of clergy sexual abuse of minors at quickly assembled meetings of the response team, which included the diocese's legal officer.) On occasion, I brought to the bishop requests from priests for special considerations—a change in assignment to be closer to a sick parent, permission for extended absence from their parish assignment for graduate study and the like. How I presented these petitions could, in some instances, make a difference in the bishop's decision. A raised eyebrow, a knowing smile, could shape and color the request as well as the bishop's response. The priests, I understood, deserved my best effort on their behalf. I hope I served them well.

Later, as president-rector of our major seminary, I knew another dimension of power—the direct or indirect agency over the life of another—a candidate for admission, a seminarian's promotion to the next level of study, and most importantly, whether to recommend to the bishop a seminarian for ordination to the priesthood. I made these decisions always in consultation with and in concert with the members of the formation faculty. We discussed each seminarian under evaluation at considerable length, aware that we were involved in a prayerful, thoughtful discernment that nonetheless was an exercise of power. After listening carefully to each other, we voted, and the majority carried with few exceptions. We faculty fully understood we were in a position of power, and we tried to our very best to be fair while holding in mind what we believed was best for the church, our diocese, and the seminarian in question. It was a humbling experience—as all acts of power should be.

So, I've had a taste of power. I've seen up close its ability to do great good and the great harm it can do when abused. While it can be perverted and abused, it is in itself morally neutral and when exercised for the common good and in service to the Reign of God, it is good and necessary—and holy.

The focus of these entries will be centered, for the most part, on hierarchical power—literally the holy or sacred power of those in positions of church leadership. Sacred power, I'm convinced, is the most complex of all powers. Its origin is recognized by believers as divine while the stepping-stones to church power, though under the umbrella of the Holy Spirit's guidance, are clearly human and fraught with the conscious and unconscious dynamics of ambition as well as the exquisite subtleties of clerical culture.

————•◆•————

A PSYCHOLOGIST FRIEND AND classmate from my graduate school days, and a priest who has seen clearly into clericalism's baroque center, mentioned something in passing I've never forgotten. Catholic clergy, he observed, have to deal with two major repressions: the repression (or sublimation) of their sexual drive *and* the repression of their ambition. I knew he was on to something, for ambition's psychic energy fuels our striving for all kinds of goals and objectives from holiness to fame, from money to power. Ambition, he reminded me, is as strong and pervasive a drive as the sexual. Ambition's repression, moreover, is as tricky as any repression of the sexual impulse. It's so complicated because priests and vowed religious, by definition and common assumption, are unambitious. The only appropriate ambition for a priest or religious is the ambition to be the priest, sister, brother, nun, or monk God wants them to be. As Saint Ignatius put it, "That's enough for me."

I'm reminded here of Christmas midnight Mass at Saint Ann's Church years ago where, as vicar for priests, I was in residence. Assembled in the sacristy were the parish's best altar servers, including Robert, an exceptional young man studying, with enthusiasm, Latin and Greek, devout and responsible beyond his years. In the lull before leaving the sacristy, I asked Robert if he had thought about being a priest. "Oh no, Father," he said without hesitation. "I don't want to be a priest. I want to be a bishop."

Only one innocent of the clerical world could respond as Robert did. It's not only bad form, it's quite unthinkable for a priest to say out loud that he wants to be a bishop. The appropriate response when priests discuss their futures is, predictably, "I just want to be a good priest." Imagine a young woman presenting herself to a novice mistress, "I would like to enter this convent. But, my real desire is to be Mother Superior." Now a priest, in all humility, might believe he has what it takes to be a bishop, and a good one. There is no personnel office to which he can submit his application for ordination to the episcopacy. Nor would it work for him to meet with his bishop and declare his suitability for the office of bishop. And so clerical ambition is repressed or disguised. And as it is with all repressed drives, its bottled energy emerges or erupts in unhealthy manifestations of power or control.

It's clear that most priests don't want to be bishops although many would like to be asked. And most novices don't aspire to be Mother Superior. But for priests who do believe they are called to high office in the church, how they proceed is complicated to say the least. They must learn the unspoken clerical protocols that better their chances to catch the bishop's eye. They must find ways to call attention to their loyalty, competence, and intelligence. Their preaching must be safe, never prophetic; their pastoral work always in accord with canon law. And any books or articles they write should reflect unambiguously official church teaching. I mention all this because there is something less than honorable in this kind of ambitious maneuvering. It chips away at the priest's integrity, at his soul. And should church power be achieved, the main goal thereafter is to hold on to it.

THE PRELATES I'VE COME TO KNOW, seldom if ever, I suspect, thought of themselves as men of power or overtly aspired to positions of greater power or status. In fact, the bishop I worked rather closely with seemed genuinely uninterested in moving up the episcopal ladder. We members of his staff respected him for this. I'm generalizing here, of course, but bishops, archbishops, and cardinals, I believe, are not power-hungry men. They tend to think of themselves as servants of the church burdened with great responsibility. Yes, there have been (as history makes clear), and there are today, prelates who see themselves as members of the church's nobility (royalty?) and, by the grace of God, entitled to live as medieval princes of the church. But I can't believe that's the case with most of the men in purple and scarlet. But I should be careful here. Ecclesiastical ambition is readily disguised as a compelling drive, noble and pure, to serve the church from the highest positions of authority. The taste of power, with its privilege, status, comfort, and unquestioned expense account (the *mensa episcopalis:* the "table of the bishop") has seduced the most honorable of men. Call a clergyman "your Excellency," "your Grace," "your Eminence" often enough and he soon begins to think of himself as not like the rest of men but a man set apart by divine selection, someone entitled to the deference of the Catholic faithful. Moreover, he's accountable only to the pope and to God.

In a sense, of course, he is set apart. But it would be healthier and better for the church if a bishop thought of himself as a man set in the middle of the community, as a member of the community, charged to hold the community together by the light of the Gospel. The bishop is first, then, an agent of communion, teaching first by example how to trust that Jesus is the Christ, that God is love, that even in our darkest moments, the Spirit is in our midst.

On the local level, the office of bishop, as it has evolved since the early Middle Ages, is ultimate religious power—and a profound responsibility. In this realm of sacred power, the virtue of humility can melt like an ice cube in an August sun. When that happens, calls for transparency and accountability are taken as an affront, as rank disrespect.

> There is no spiritual life which does not
> encounter disappointment and disillusionment,
> suffering and confusion.

> — Jean Sulivan

Power to Hold

THE SOURCE OF ALL CHURCH POWER, from popes to pastors, from mothers superior to novices, from lay ministers to people in the pews, is, we know, the Holy Spirit. And church power is always, at heart, pastoral power. It's power given for the care and flourishing of God's people. Church power, in all its forms, is meant to hold us in harmony with God's unseen order. It isn't willful; it isn't controlling. It is slow to condemn and slow to excommunicate. Rather, it's meant to hold us in God's mercy. It's meant to hold us in Christ's arms where we experience the healing touch and feel the breath of the divine. That's at the heart of the church's power—to gather and to hold, to tell again and again the story of God's fidelity, to break the bread and share the cup.

In other words, the church's power is meant to hold us in truth and goodness and the sublime beauty of the Gospel. To accomplish this, the church has teaching power that deserves our respect and attention. But the church's teaching power is communicated best by humble words and compelling witness to the truth, not by the sheer force of authority. As I mentioned earlier, thinking Catholics no longer take dictation. Their first obedience is to the Gospel and their conscience to which they hold dearly. This, they understand, is holding fast to their faith.

It appears most bishops take seriously their responsibility, that is, power, to hold us in communion. It must be a staggering task in our complex, fractured, and secular world. I suspect many feel anything but men of power. In fact they must feel powerless a good deal of the time. Paddling upstream against currents of Catholic outrage at their public failures, they struggle to sustain the "serious conversation that leads to blessed communion." Other bishops, I'm afraid, aren't interested in conversation, serious or otherwise. After all, they believe they hold the absolute, God-given truth. These prelates, certainly not all, are more interested in mounting their pulpits to declare the truth to shrinking congregations. But they have missed an important step. They must first listen—by entering into conversation with the flock— before they can teach effectively and hold their people in communion and hold their attention. So bishops and all preachers, ordained and lay, "listen," in the sense of participative discernment, for the questions, concerns, and anxieties that parishioners bring to worship. Often these matters of the heart are implicit, not fully conscious, but they remain the human hungers that in some manner or other affect us all. The Word of God, then, in the mouth of the preacher, has the power to come alive with a kind of electricity creating a holy circuit between the Spirit and the congregation. Inspiring, challenging, prophetic preaching falls like a beam of sunlight when the bearer of the Word communicates to the assembly that he or she understands their joys and sorrows, their struggles and fears, their hopes and desires.

I'm thinking here of the French writer, Jean Sulivan, who wrote the following about bishops' preaching:

The hierarchy . . . had, it believed, to take into account many things. It was a little cross-eyed. One eye was on the tiny fringe of the faithful who surrounded the bishops and prevented them from seeing the crowd; another was on Rome, which insisted that the Word be preached

but was no longer open to conversion by it, because Rome itself had a monopoly on all its
meanings.[21]

THEN SULIVAN ADDS, "During my active service as a
priest, I have assisted and participated in the humiliation
of the Word, both within me and outside of me, to the
profit of ideologies and sentiments." Preachers, myself in
particular, feel a twinge in their stomachs reading that
stark sentence. How we have abused the power of the
Word in our sermons and homilies! Sulivan is right; we
never really break free of our theologies (ideologies) and
pieties (sentiments). Perhaps completely breaking free is
simply impossible.

> Now that I am a priest I have a boundless
> capacity for thwarting good—
> and for turning wine into water.

> — Anonymous

FOR ONLY A HANDFUL OF YEARS, Angelo Giuseppe Ron-
calli, the beloved and now blessed John XXIII, knew
how to hold the church in communion. In his jovial
girth, he appeared to take the world into his arms. He
knew how to comfort and heal, but he obviously knew
how to challenge and lead. In a history-changing act of
church power, the pope called for an Ecumenical Council. And for a handful of years, Vatican II held the hopes

of multitudes of Catholics for a renewed, more humble, more open to the world church. Other powers—controlling, willful, fear driven—we now see are at work rescinding John's Council. Power struggles, no matter how sacred or sincere, are shaking to its core the church's communion.

There's evidence that John XXIII understood that the calling of an Ecumenical Council would spark fierce power struggles. Thomas Cahill, in his *Pope John XXIII*, reports a revealing exchange between Pope John and his close friend and secretary, Don Loris Capovilla. Confiding to his friend his intention to call a Council, Capovilla implored him not to. He warned the pope that the Council would be met with strong opposition from members of the Vatican Curia and was doomed to fail. After considering his friend's counsel for a few days, John said to him, "The trouble is, Don Loris, that you're still not detached enough from self—you're still concerned with having a good reputation." Then, as if he had read of Thomas Merton's insight into the false self, the pope continued, "Only when the ego has been trampled underfoot can one be fully and truly free. You are not yet free, Don Loris." Power in the hands of those who are not spiritually free and authentically humble is dangerous. If we look closely, we see it is self-serving, manipulative, and deceitful. Not just some of the time, but almost all the time. So show me the spiritually free and authentically humble. . . . And, thus, the state of our church and world.

> Power tends to corrupt; absolute
> power corrupts absolutely.
>
> — Lord John Acton

IF THERE IS A TIME TO HOLD, there is also a time to let go. And here, I believe, we confront one of the many paradoxes of power. For those in power (I'm thinking primarily of those holding church power), the ability to let go—the virtue of detachment—is critical. If you can't let go of the power you possess, if you can't surrender it gracefully when it is time to do so, you will most likely abuse it. Those who exercise power well are always detached from it—in the sense of not making it their personal power. Pope John XXIII had this power of detachment. And this was the core of his spiritual freedom and his power to act with such courage and confidence. He let go of his fear that the Council might fail, that he might be making a terrible mistake in calling it. In his *The Journal of a Soul*, John revealed that he treasured the maxim, "Absolute trust in God in the present and complete tranquility in regard to what is going to happen in the future." He was free, even of the power of the papacy.

If we remain attached to anything—our possessions, our self-image, our security, the need to control—our exercise of power will always be perilous for others and inevitably for ourselves.

Power to Lead

I HAVE THE IMPRESSION THAT prelates understand their power primarily as a power to guard and protect. They see it as the responsibility to safeguard the Deposit of Faith (Beliefs), to protect the credibility and authority of the teaching office of the church, to ensure the order and discipline required for a world religion, and to protect the faithful from errors and heresies likely to harm their "simple faith." Their evangelical and pastoral responsibilities, on the other hand, while remaining close to the center of their ministry, take a second place in terms of time and energy to the "sentinel duties" of guarding and protecting. We shouldn't be surprised. It is so with all institutional leadership. Guarding and protecting are defensive powers—powers that certainly have their place in the leadership of the church. But they remain dangerous powers in the sense that they tend to place the viability and strength of the institution as institution ahead of the people the institution is meant to serve. And in the case of the church, its prelates' fears of scandal— read here the tarnishing of the public image of bishops and priests—have led not only to denials, dissimulations, minimizations, but to patterns and structures of secrecy that have caused greater scandals than they were intended to hide.

Examples of this sentinel mode of leadership abound; none more shocking, even sickening, than the cover-up of priest abusers of minors and children by numerous bishops throughout the world. Their fear of scandal led not to the multiplication of safe havens for the vulnerable, but to the multiplication of innocent victims for pederast priests and bishops. All for "the good of the church."

BUT THE CHURCH IS NOT FUNDAMENTALLY a Fort Knox of revealed truths and dogmas that must be defended from its enemies at all costs. Let the Vatican post its sentinels. But let Rome and the bishops of the world support and encourage "trail guides" for a church that is more a pilgrimage of God's holy people than an institution. And let Rome give us real food for the journey rather than arid propositions requiring obsequience and convoluted, arcane prayers for our liturgies. Let Rome give us leaders—or better, let us raise up leaders—who have walked the trail, who understand our fears and struggles, who encourage and lift up rather than reprimand and control. And let us recognize and celebrate the unofficial trail guides—parish and family elders, teachers, counselors—commissioned by the rite of baptism, whose leadership and holding powers have kept the pilgrim people on track down through the ages.

I'm thankful for the trail guides that offered direction, inspiration, and hope to me along the way. I mention here but a few more or less contemporaries: writers Eugene Kennedy, Joan Chittister, Richard Rohr, and Paul Wilkes; theologians Paul Tillich, Charles Curran, Elizabeth Johnson, Richard McBrien, Thomas O'Meara, Mary Catherine Hilkert, and Robert Krieg; Cardinals Joseph Bernardin, Roger Mahony, and Carlo Martini; Archbishops Oscar Romero, Rembert Weakland, Rowan Williams, and Desmond Tutu; Bishops Geoffrey Robinson, P. Frank Murphy, Kenneth Untner, Thomas Gumbleton, Matthew Clark, Raymond Lucker, Donald Trautman, and Robert Morneau; my family and a precious circle of wise friends. In one fashion or another, I turn to one or more of these trail guides almost every day. They are light to my feet.

WITHOUT QUESTION, THE MINISTRY of prophecy is the most dangerous element of leadership—dangerous not only because of those who see Christianity as the enemy, but dangerous because of members of the church who see any calls for renewal, reform, or the development of official teaching as a threat to the strength and well-being of the church. Most prophets are without honor, not only in their own country, but anywhere and everywhere. It's especially dangerous in totalitarian systems, understandably, but prophetic leadership is still risky in democracies and institutions like the church.

I've already described Pope John's decision to call an Ecumenical Council courageous. Never did the rather round pontiff stand more straight and tall than when he announced his prophetic decision to a startled and alarmed Vatican Curia and to a surprised and hopeful Catholic world. He stood in good company. Facing the rank injustices of the Industrial Revolution and its barons—the Rockefellers, Carnegies, Krupps, and Nobels—Pope Leo XIII issued in 1891 his encyclical *Rerum Novarum*, the Magna Carta of social Catholicism. Our papal prophets have been at their courageous best when proclaiming the Gospel values of justice and peace in an age of unparalleled violence, greed, and worker exploitation—from Leo XIII to Benedict XV to Pius XI, to John XXIII, to John Paul II. And, I must add that one of the champions of English workers in the late nineteenth century was Cardinal Henry Edward Manning, the arch-enemy of the famed Cardinal John Henry Newman.

In my own day, before the Vatican's neutering of the United States Conference of Catholic Bishops (they must now achieve a unanimous vote or the Vatican's approval before issuing teaching letters or policy statements as a Conference), the American bishops issued two truly prophetic pastoral letters, *The Challenge of Peace* and *Economic Justice for All*. And to their credit, they continue to speak forcefully in defense of human life, especially of the unborn, and to a number of social issues such as immigration laws, religious freedom, and sexual trafficking.

We priests have our prophets—the Jesuit martyrs of El Salvador and the Berrigan brothers, among others. But by and large, we are regarded primarily for our sentinel and pastoral ministry. Understandable in one light. We mostly have forgotten the labor priests of the early and middle twentieth century. Moreover, many of us ordained during and just after the Council didn't have specific courses on Catholic social teaching, nor was it a priority in the seminary curriculum. And our current corps of seminarians comes mostly from middle-class rather than working-class families. (Could this be a factor in the precipitous plunge in the number of candidates preparing for the priesthood? When our seminaries were bursting at the seams, most of the seminarians were from working-class families.) Prophetic preaching sometimes leads to applause. But more often, pastors say that it divides the parish and results in calls of complaint to the chancery. Priests, like most of us, like to be liked. And we prefer calm waters. Prophetic preaching and teaching always rock the boat.

We preachers, for the most part, have made compromises with our secular and materialistic culture. The line between prudent and cowardly compromises is often unclear. And we preachers have made compromises with some church teachings with which we disagree—is every deliberate sexual thought or desire always a mortal sin? Can missing one Mass on Sunday lead to an eternity in hell? Are spouses with children risking the salvation of their souls by practicing artificial birth control? Is a gay son or a lesbian daughter objectively disordered? Most priests would say it's better to handle issues like these on the pastoral level—not in the pulpit. Are these compromises with church teaching prudent? In most cases, I believe so.

Perhaps in another light, our pastoral prudence, our holding our cards close to our vests, is less than honorable. We priests need to wrestle with that.

WE SHOULDN'T BE PROUD OF THIS, though many Catholics are, that the church is the last absolute monarchy in the West. Some loyalists see the church as a spiritual empire, whole in itself, perfect unto itself, an "eternal now" standing outside and above history. Everything has already been given and contained in the sacred deposit. There can be, therefore, no real newness because everything essential is already possessed. Wherever that is the case, whether in Rome or Paris or New York, prophets live in danger. Prophecy, from any voice, from any quarter, is not only unwelcome, it's dubbed dissent and impudent.

Moreover, the church's power structure remains fundamentally feudal. In fact, the church is the last true feudal system in the West. The pope, naturally, is the sovereign and he bequeaths benefices to his lords; the bishops dutifully send to their sovereign financial sums for the sovereign's court, the operating expenses of the Vatican, and for the church's considerable charitable works. The bishops, in turn, bequeath benefices, that is, parishes, to their priests who faithfully (for the most part) send the assigned assessments (taxes, if you will) to the bishop for the maintenance of the diocesan chancery and to support the many charitable and other good works of the diocese.

Loyalty has always been the glue that holds any feudal system in place. The track is clear: loyalty of the vassal bishop to the pope; loyalty of the vassal pastor to his bishop. In this context, prophetic leadership or prophetic preaching can be daunting.

The church's feudal system has worked well for centuries, but it doesn't work in the modern world where the serfs—the laity—happen to be in many cases better educated than their pastors and bishops. Catholics refuse to remain patient and docile in the absence of accountability (in a feudal system accountability is always and exclusively upward—pastor to bishop, bishop to pope) and transparency concerning finances and the processes leading to major decisions that affect their lives. In this milieu, calls from the laity for accountability and transparency fall on many bishops' ears as rank disrespect. Bishops can't say this out loud, but I think many of them say to themselves, "Don't you trust me?" "Do princes owe accountability and transparency to their subjects?" While this episcopal attitude may not be common, it's common enough to have tragically compounded the clergy sexual abuse scandals.

Moreover, the church's feudal structure's disregard for accountability and transparency encourages all forms of financial abuse and corruption. It's true that recent financial scandals involving the Vatican bank and its networks of cooperating banks and investment houses have led to previously unheard-of systems of oversight and supervision. Here, too, prophetic calls for reform are resisted. Too many private benefices and fiefdoms would be exposed.

The Power of Witness

A PROPHET AROSE IN THE FIRST QUARTER of the twentieth century who feared neither bishop nor police chief, though she raised the ire of both. Dorothy Day knew in her heart what the Gospel asked of her and she acted and wrote accordingly. Now, officially acclaimed as a "Servant of God" (the first step leading to canonization), her early resume includes ambitious journalist, Communist sympathizer, passionate lover, unwed mother—and finally convert to Catholicism. Like Saint Augustine, her heart was restless until it rested in the hold of Christ's love. Then she tried, to the point of exhaustion, to hold the poor of Manhattan and the world in her arms. And to a remarkable extent, she succeeded. To the surprise of some, Day is acclaimed by critics as America's most outstanding Catholic writer. More significantly, she may be America's most outstanding Catholic prophet.

Her life, her heroic ministry, and her writings certainly pricked the consciences of a broad swath of Americans. She made some of the hierarchy uncomfortable—was she taking this passion for social justice too far?—but the power of her witness made her more or less untouchable. Dorothy Day's autobiography, *The Long Loneliness*, and her *Catholic Worker* columns stand today as profoundly and courageously prophetic.

MY SEMINARY CLASSMATE, Bernie Meyer, has been a social activist and Gospel witness for half a century now. He's been arrested numerous times, has done time in jail, and continues to witness and lecture both here and abroad against nuclear weapons and for social justice and a green earth. He's as poor and brave and steadfast as Dorothy Day. At a breakfast with the "coffee house theologians" not long ago, his calm eyes and measured voice reflected a soul in harmony with the unseen order. There is no hint of anger in Bernie. No hint of judgment. Like all true prophets and witnesses, he lives in the presence of God.

Students from John Carroll University and from schools across the country demonstrate annually in Washington,

D.C., for the repeal of *Roe vs. Wade*. And many of the
same students travel each spring to Fort Benning, Geor-
gia, to protest at the former School of the Americas,
where thousands of Central and South American soldiers have been trained by the U.S. military in counter-
insurgency tactics that reportedly show little regard for
fundamental human rights. Their witness, unlike Bernie
Meyer's, is hardly radical, but it is authentic. Their goodness, idealism, and generosity give me hope.

ABOVE MY DESK IN MY JOHN CARROLL office is a pic-
ture of Dorothy and Jean, two young Cleveland women
in identical bright orange Salvadoran blouses. They are
standing shoulder to shoulder in an afternoon sun; their
smiles are easy and genuine. One would never think they
were so close to their deaths. Ursuline Sister Dorothy
Kazel, lay missionary Jean Donovan, and Maryknoll
Sisters Maura Clarke and Ita Ford were kidnapped outside the San Salvador Airport in December of 1980 by
National Guard soldiers, driven into the hills to a desert-
ed roadside clearing, and without mercy and I suspect
without hesitation, were raped and then shot to death.

I didn't know Dorothy Kazel well although we
moved in the same circles, and I was teaching at the time
of her murder at Ursuline College, which is sponsored by
her congregation. I did, however, know her brother, Jim,
well—we played tennis regularly—and her sister-in-law,

Dorothy. Sister Dorothy's nieces were students of mine at the college. And I remember her parents, Malvina and Joseph, who bore their unspeakable grief with quiet dignity. When I was with Jim in the days after the news of his sister's brutal death, I sensed the building outrage in his chest. He was ready to act (I will not say how). We spoke in whispers about the immense obstacles he would surely encounter.

I believe I understood Jim Kazel's raw rage for revenge, for justice. To that I had nothing to say. Years later, we heard that those responsible for the murders lived comfortably in Florida.

> Those who teach justice shall be
> like the stars forever.
>
> — Daniel 12:3

LESS THAN A DECADE LATER, in November of 1989, nine Jesuits were ordered by National Guard soldiers from their faculty residence on the campus of the University of Central America in El Salvador, and made to lie face down on the grassy area adjacent to the home. Then, with military precision, they were each shot in the back of the head with high-powered American-made rifles. The soldiers also shot to death the Jesuits' cook and her teenage daughter. On one of my visits to El Salvador, in the company of two missionaries from Cleveland,

I stood on the lawn—holy ground—where the Jesuits were executed. Rose bushes have been planted there, as if to be nourished by the Jesuits' blood. No one spoke. I walked inside the residence—there were bullet holes in the walls of the small room where their cook and her daughter were murdered. I was standing in a holy place. I should have run my hands over the pockmarked walls and knelt to kiss the floor.

I wanted to be alone. I wanted to sit alone in the Jesuits' chapel. There was no feeling. Not for the first few minutes anyway. Something was keeping the crushing wave of sadness at bay so I could taste the bitter void of evil.

So this is what prophecy and ministry can lead to. Not for most of us, of course, but for some. And we're not free to do the final sorting.

BEFORE LEAVING EL SALVADOR, I heard a bizarre story from one of the missionaries who was associated with the murdered Jesuits. It's hearsay, but it has the ring of truth. The decision to murder the Jesuits, who were writing and teaching on social justice in the midst of El Salvador's civil war, was made late at night at a large conference table. A dozen or so military leaders sat around the table. It was agreed that the Jesuits were a threat to the stability of the right-wing government and had to be eliminated. The colonel in charge turned to a younger officer and told him he was to lead a squad of soldiers to execute the order. The junior officer requested to be relieved, explaining that he had been a student of one of the Jesuits and would find carrying out the order to kill his former professor and the others difficult. The colonel ignored the plea.

Then, the officers all stood, I was told, joined hands, and prayed the *Padre Nuestra*, the Our Father.

RELIGION'S POWER, WE KNOW, is a precarious power, easily compromised by misguided efforts to protect its institutions from the encroachments of governments or secular societies. Still, under the banner of the Cross and in the name of the Christ and his Gospel we have defended the poor and exploited of our world, worked for justice and peace, pointed to the spirit-sapping thrust of materialism and consumerism, and condemned nuclear proliferation. Through Catholic Relief Services, we have been among the first responders to the victims of earthquakes, hurricanes, and tsunamis. We have, arguably, the best network of schools, social service ministries, and hospitals in the world. Much of this immense good— I'm tempted to say most—has come from the devotion, dedication, and expertise of Catholic sisters. The head of the church may be in Rome, but the heart of the church is in the barrios, classrooms, orphanages, and hospitals where sisters and brothers, lay ministers and missionaries, priests and deacons serve quietly and faithfully.

But under this same banner and in the name of Christ we have had our dark moments. Our history, as the Crusades and our Inquisitions reveal, has not always been honorable. We have forced baptism on tribes and peoples, behaved at times with the ruthlessness of the Mafia, and matched the callous corruptions of our secular society. And for "the good of the church," we've turned our backs on the victims of clergy sexual abuse while turning our attention to the paid-for counsel of lawyers and public relations gurus. In these matters and countless others, our misuse and abuse of power has left us with blood on our hands.

The abuse of power that has touched the lives of most Catholics, however, falls in the category of ecclesiastical "misdemeanors." It can easily be dismissed as simply part of the human condition. Pastors—both bishops and priests—guilty of unkindness, guilty of legalisms that place the letter of the law above the spirit of the law, and guilty of arrogant self-righteousness, wound the church and discredit its liberating teaching and teaching authority. Without denying the immense good we see in the church, I'm scandalized by its capacity for meanness—a meanness we've seen erupt lately in a number of Rome's abrasive critiques and condemnations of her creative theologians, her faithful religious, and prophetic priests.

>   Smugness is the great Catholic sin.

>   — Flannery O'Connor

LOOKING AT THE CHURCH TODAY, especially its short-sightedness toward women, its concern for dogma over spirituality, its reluctance to critique itself, its unraveling of Vatican II, I wonder—and struggle—with my place in it all. I turn again to the lines from of the poet, Kilian McDonnell, that so disturb me: "No grand betrayals / we lacked the impudent will / we died of small treasons." Just how guilty am I of small treasons? Just how guilty am I of cowardly compromises that I rationalize as prudent compromises? Just how guilty am I of going along to get along? It's hard to know. I've been conditioned to please, to be the "good priest." Still, there's no denying, in spite of the hope I find in my students, that I'm discouraged and weary. I trace much of this feeling of underground dislocation to the realization that the pilgrim church has been forcibly tucked inside the garrison walls of the Roman Catholic Church. As such, it's going nowhere.

So, I think I know how the Jesuit paleontologist Pierre Teilhard de Chardin felt when he wrote the following lines in one of his letters:

>   I no longer have confidence in the exterior mani-
>   festations of the church. I believe that through it

the divine influence will continue to reach me,
but I no longer have much belief in the immediate and tangible value of official directions and
decisions.

Some people feel happy in the visible church;
but for my own part I think I shall be happy
to die in order to be free of it—and to find our
Lord outside of it.

IMAGINATION

————•◆•————

THE WRITTEN WORD MAY CAPTURE the workings of imagination, but it also tends to lock these workings into rational forms that suppress or weaken their energy and creativity. I think Jesus understood this. That's why he didn't direct his disciples who could write to take down his sermons. Could it be that Jesus didn't give dictation because he understood there would be disputes over what he said, how accurately it was recorded, and how it was to be interpreted? Perhaps he believed there would be fewer disputes with an oral tradition for the first decades after his Resurrection rather than texts of his preaching scribbled by scribes. But I shouldn't be surprised. Jesus preached a radical new way of living rather than a set of doctrines to be memorized and attested to as the definitive sign of faith. But assent to doctrines, as I noted earlier in this journal, is easier to measure than faith as trust in God's loving compassion and abiding presence. Sadly, it's belief in doctrines rather than faith in the triune God and the Way of the Gospel that defines us Christians and crystallizes our identity. It should be the other way around.

I continue to struggle to make sense out of the ruptures the church suffers over doctrinal disputes. Faith in God, in the Christ, in the Spirit, apparently aren't enough common ground to unite the Orthodox Church and the Catholic Church. We have so much in common, but we allow doctrinal disputes to divide us. Should the *filioque*—how the Spirit proceeds from the other persons of the Trinity—keep us divided? The theologians and bishops tell me it's much more complicated than whether the Spirit proceeded from the Father and Son rather than from the Father through the Son. Of course it is—there are other factors: theological, political, and historical in the mix—but surely the Spirit is inspiring our imaginations to work out this scandalous division over issues that are not, from my point of view, ultimate or central to the Gospel. I fear we have locked up our imaginations inside the vault of the Deposit of Beliefs.

I WRITE THIS ENTRY ON THE 11TH OF OCTOBER, 2012, fifty years to the day of the opening of the Second Vatican Council. October 11, 1962, marks the great emancipation of the church's imagination which had been held under lock and key since the Council of Trent. And so imagine a church that truly respected the Spirit's freedom to bestow her gifts—her charisms—where she pleased, on whom she pleased. I can't imagine the Spirit decreeing that gifts of ministry and of orders will be restricted to males only. I can't imagine the Spirit limiting the charism of preaching and priesthood to males only. I can't imagine this because I've been moved to tears at the preaching of women and their gifts of presiding. And I've been moved to silent weeping at the didactic, uninspiring preaching and mechanical presiding of many priests.

Can we imagine an unfettered Spirit? Can we imagine the Spirit blessing and charging both women and men to preach the Gospel and shepherd the church? There lies the future church.

THE CHURCH IS WIDELY CRITICIZED today, even by those who know it well and still find nourishment at its table. There are painful and often accurate accusations of hypocrisy, duplicity, authoritarianism, triumphalism, and corruption rising up not only from the secular city, but also from loyal, life-long Catholics who desire a healthier and holier church. I count myself among those faithful hanging on and hoping for signs of renewal. And to buoy my spirits I try to imagine a renewed and reformed church, a church faithful to the Gospel yet humble and compassionate. I try to imagine a church that relies on the power of its witness more than its proclamations, declarations, and instructions to proclaim the liberating spirit of Jesus. I try to imagine a church that is truly inclusive, that sees into the fundamental equality of the men and women who make up the people of God. I try to imagine a church that our secular world respects and is ready to engage because it rings loud and true with authenticity and integrity.

Here's the irony as I see it. As our "secular city" becomes more and more superficial and spiritually bankrupt, it is likely to discover and acknowledge the despair it has been fostering by its unbridled materialism, consumerism, and hedonism. When the pendulum does eventually swing in the opposite direction, large numbers of people will be looking for a way out, for some way to escape the sickness that has taken over their lives. The Catholic Church, with other faith-based communions, will be poised to offer a word from the Lord, the saving paradox of the Paschal Mystery. But only if we ourselves live by the word we proclaim. I fear we are not yet credible enough as a church to be taken seriously. The present beam of our light is too weak to be a trustworthy beacon. I'm afraid we will miss our moment.

> We have reached a point where we
> can no longer rely on institutions.

— The Dalai Lama speaking to Thomas Merton

IMAGINE THIS. AN INTERNATIONALLY televised Pontifical Mass in St. Peter's Basilica where half of the altar servers are young women and girls. And prominent among the mitered bishops in the sanctuary are the women major superiors of the religious orders with headquarters in Rome. Among the male deacons ministering at the Basilica's high altar we observe women deacons. The congregation rises for the Gospel acclamation and a woman deacon proclaims the Gospel—and preaches the homily—naming God's grace and power to lift up the powerless and downtrodden, a homily that speaks of God's humility even as the assembly worships in the baroque splendor of Catholicism's mother church. Imagine that.

IMAGINE THIS. THE VATICAN PRESS OFFICE releases a Pontifical Letter to the Catholic world in which the pope names four women to the College of Cardinals—representing Asia, Africa, the Americas, and Europe. While withholding ordination either as priests or bishops, the pope has granted the newly named cardinals full voting rights at the next Papal Conclave. Imagine that.

IMAGINE THIS. THE VATICAN PRESS OFFICE announces that a leaked report of a secret committee of theologians and canon lawyers convened by the pope to determine if an apparent theological problem in Canon 277 needs to be corrected. Canon 277 requires celibacy for Latin rite priests and reads: "Clerics are obliged to observe perfect and perpetual continence for the sake of the kingdom of heaven and therefore are obliged to observe celibacy, which is a special gift of God, by which sacred ministers can adhere more easily to Christ with an undivided heart and can more freely dedicate themselves to the service of God and humankind."

The theologians and canonists were instructed to determine if it is within the discretionary power of the church to legislate a gift—or charism—from God. The canon states explicitly that celibacy is "a special gift from God." Does the church have the right to propose that God will bestow the special gift of celibacy on every candidate for the Latin rite priesthood? Furthermore, does the church have the power to mandate celibacy for Latin rite priests if it is a gift? The committee concluded that the church does have the right to require celibacy, as it has for Latin rite priests since the twelfth century, but that it is theologically problematic and possibly arrogant for the church to claim it knows upon whom this gift will be bestowed. The canonists recommended to the pope that if he wished to maintain the discipline of celibacy for the Latin rite, the phrase, "which is a special gift from God," should be deleted from Canon 277. They further recommended that if the pope was convinced that celibacy is indeed a gift from God, then it should be left to the individual seminarian to prayerfully discern if he has been blessed with this charism. From this perspective, clerical celibacy should not be canonically imposed for the simple reason that gifts cannot be imposed by legislation.

The committee, it was noted, daringly raised a theological question that was clearly outside the charge given it by the pope. Is it not possible that God would grant to an individual a vocation to both the sacrament of orders and to the sacrament of marriage? Apparently God did precisely this for most of the church's two-thousand-year history. In a lengthy footnote, the committee noted that many married popes (there were at least thirty-nine) were acclaimed saints of the church. Pope St. Anastasius I (399–401), moreover, was succeeded by his son, Pope St. Innocent I (401–417). A century later, Pope St. Hormisdas (514–523) fathered a son who became Pope St. Silverius (536–537). Finally, the committee pointed to still another papal lineage of sorts—Pope Gregory the Great (590–604) was the great-grandson of Pope Felix III and the great-great-grandson of Pope Felix II. Imagine that.

Let me add a postscript. Our imaginary committee concluded its report by noting that Canon 277 was, unfortunately, a tautology—a statement that is true by its own definition and is therefore fundamentally uninformative (e.g., lying is wrong because it is a sin). The canon reads, "Clerics are obliged to observe perfect and perpetual continence for the sake of the kingdom of heaven (an assertion and an assumption) and therefore are obliged to observe celibacy"(an assertion). For those of us who see the canon as logically contorted, it comes down to this—it is so because the church says it is so.

Before the curtain comes down on this fictitious scenario, the cardinal prefect of the Congregation for the
Clergy issues a statement that the leaked report of the
committee should not be taken as an indication of any
change in the church's long-standing tradition and practice of clerical celibacy.

IMAGINE THIS. THE VATICAN sponsors an international
symposium of the world's most distinguished moral
theologians to review the church's theology of human
sexuality. More than half of the symposium's participants are lay, married scholars. Speaker after speaker
criticizes the "act-centered" approach to sexual ethics
that has held sway in Catholic circles for centuries. The
majority of theologians propose that the fundamental
criteria for taking the moral measure of sexual behavior
should be to determine if it's loving, respectful, mutual,
and life-giving. From this perspective, the theologians
question the current teaching that every sexual behavior,
fantasy, or desire outside of marriage is always objectively mortally sinful.

The participants applaud the church's teaching office for affirming that, by its very nature, "sex makes
promises," that casual and recreational sex negates the
spiritual and bonding potential of loving sexuality in
marriage. The symposium members are unanimous in

condemning the violence of sexual abuse, sexual trafficking, and all forms of exploitation of children, women, and men. Finally, the symposium participants recommend that the pope establish a special commission to review the teaching that all forms of artificial contraception are always intrinsically evil. Imagine that.

> Oh Rome, Rome, be converted
> and turn to the Lord thy God.
>
> — St. Bridget of Sweden

RECENTLY I CAME ACROSS A PASSAGE in Leo Tolstoy's *War and Peace* that made me think of the men chosen to be bishops. Prince Andrei, one of the novel's protagonists, has seen Russia's generals in action and is bemused that many of the Russian nobility think they are geniuses. Sitting in the company of a number of generals, Andrei thinks,

A good general does not need genius or special qualities of any kind, on the contrary, what he requires is the absence of the very finest, highest human qualities—love, poetry, tenderness, philosophical, enquiring doubt. He has to be limited and firmly believe that what he does is very important, otherwise he will not have the patience for it. Only then will he be a good general. God

forbid that he should be a man who falls in love
with anyone, feels sorry for anyone, or starts
thinking about what is just and what is not.[22]

Good bishops like good generals don't have to be
geniuses, but they serve far better if they do possess the
"very finest, highest human qualities." We need bishops
(and generals) who love poetry, read widely, and love
music—*and think critically and creatively*. Without these
qualities, imagination withers and leadership is reduced
to the maintenance of discipline and doctrine. On the
contrary, Prince Andrei, we need bishops (and generals)
who are capable of falling in love with someone—one
of the surest, purest signs of graced humanity—who feel
sorry for others, and who start thinking about what is
just and what is not.

WE NEED BISHOPS LIKE Carlo Maria Martini, the cardinal archbishop of Milan who died in August of 2012.
Just weeks before he died, he gave a prophetic, no-holds-
barred interview that was to be published only after his
death. It appeared almost immediately, before his funer-
al, in fact, in the Italian daily, *Corriere della Sera*. "The
church is 200 years out of date," Martini said. "Why
don't we rouse ourselves? Are we afraid?" I can't recall
such directness from a high-ranking prelate. "Our culture has aged, our churches are big and empty and the

church bureaucracy rises up, our rituals and our cassocks are pompous." Then, speaking with the power of prophetic leadership, the Cardinal said, "The Church must admit its mistakes and begin a radical change, starting from the pope and the bishops. The pedophilia scandals oblige us to take a journey of transformation."

Yes, we are afraid, Cardinal Martini. And we are paying the price for our lack of trust and courage.

> Spirit is very strange,
> it has an obligation to create.

> — Mircea Eliade

ONE OF THE MARKS OF A MATURE person is the capacity for self-criticism. It follows that a mature institution would be capable of self-criticism. It seems to me that the Catholic Church abhors self-criticism as something that would weaken its credibility and moral authority. Not that long ago, Catholics were taught that their church was a perfect society, not only the "one, true, Church," but a perfect society. Perfect societies not only need not bother with self-criticism, they need not bother with renewal or reform. The Second Vatican Council apparently adjusted that understanding when the Council fathers declared that the church, as a pilgrim church, was indeed in need of renewal and reform. When we do hear words of self-criticism, the church is criticizing the faults and sins of its members, not the faults and sins of the church as church. I remember when Pope John Paul II issued *Tertio Millennio Adveniente*, he called for a thorough Catholic examination of conscience. "It is appropriate," the Pope wrote, "that as the Second Millennium of Christianity draws to a close, the Church should become more fully conscious of the sinfulness of her children, recalling all those times in history when they departed from the Spirit of Christ." In other words, the "parent" church—the pope, cardinals, and bishops—does not sin, but the "children" church—those outside the hierarchic circle—do. For the sins of its children, John Paul apologized again and again, more often than any pope in history. But for the sins of the parent—the sins of the Holy Office, the Inquisition, the sins of bishops who placed the welfare of the "church as such" ahead of the safety of her children—there was no *mea culpa*.

The following lines from the Lutheran theologian, Paul Tillich, brought me up short. "If the church does not subject itself to the judgment which is pronounced by the church, it becomes idolatrous towards itself. Such idolatry is its permanent temptation. . . . A church which tries to exclude itself from such a judgment loses its right to judge the world and is rightly judged by the world." Then he added the painful truth, "This is the tragedy of the Roman Catholic Church."[23] Yes, it is our tragedy. And we can't seem to move beyond it.

Like it or not, the Catholic Church is indeed being judged by the world. On a number of counts—the handling of the sexual abuse scandals being one of the most flagrant—the judgment is correct. Instead of a humble, *mea culpa,* many bishops fend off the world's judgment as anti-Catholic bigotry enabled by a liberal, secular media, and dissident members of the faithful. The real tragedy is that our world desperately needs the light and judgment of the Gospel. But if we don't turn the light and judgment of the Gospel on ourselves, we will continue to be judged by the world—and found unworthy of trust and bankrupt of moral authority.

> There is one spiritual lesson and
> we learn it over and over.
>
> — Catherine Mowry LaCugna

A FINAL THOUGHT ON THIS CHURCH I strive to understand and love.

I'm not sure when it began, perhaps in the fourth century with the enshrinement of our creeds—certainly by the time of the emergence of Christendom in the early Middle Ages. It was confirmed for centuries to come at the Council of Trent. Somewhere, somehow, against the core of the Gospel and the intention of Christ, the church placed on its shoulders an ideological cloak. Ideologies, as I refer to them here, are systems of thought, belief, and values that are so deeply engrained in the minds and psyches of a human collective that they are assumed to be beyond questioning, beyond expanding, beyond critiquing—and especially beyond dissent. Ideologies are closed systems that brook no opposition. Ideologues instinctively understand that imagination is their strongest enemy. And imagination is to the soul what oxygen is to the brain.

It's now early fall during a presidential election year. Two of our nation's most entrenched ideologies, the Democratic and Republican political parties, are at war. Both parties are behaving just like ideologies usually behave. Each party's political, domestic, and economic policies and platforms are beyond challenge from their own constituencies. Assaults, political and personal, are the stuff of each party's strategy. Attack ads, broad generalizations, often callously deceitful or blatantly false, stoke the public's fears and insecurities and obscure the honest differences that might help citizens to vote wisely and responsibly. As the campaign plods on, the human and spiritual pathology of these two ideologies becomes painfully clear. The possibility of reasoned arguments and civil discourse evaporates like dew in the morning sun. Especially during their respective conventions, the parties' faithful erupt into unabashed, unquestioning, and adolescent paroxysms of mindless glee. It's not only the pathology of ideology laid bare, but also the pathology of spectacle.

To the extent that the church's belief system takes on ideological strains, it's not healthy. When this is the case, prelates will put the hierarchic church ahead of the pilgrim church. To the extent that the church behaves like an ideology, it will maintain inquisitions in one form or anther and fear open dialogue and the creative insights of its theologians. And sadly, it will be incapable of judging itself by the light of the Gospel.

The church, of course, has a right to be sick, to be broken and wounded. It's human after all. It will never be perfect—as we pilgrims will never be perfect. We are naïve to expect that one day it will achieve perfection. So it deserves our patient compassion. It also deserves our best efforts to bring about healing and wholeness. But the church doesn't have the right to turn the freedom and light of the Gospel into a closed system entrenched in a medieval, feudal, and fortified castle. Pope John understood this, and he did his best to break the strains of ideology he saw compromising the church's mission. To our dismay, his opened windows are being shut and shuttered one after another.

THIS HIERARCHIC CHURCH OF ours is still learning how to live in our secular world. Christendom is long gone and with it Catholic hegemony in Europe and beyond. We're slowly catching on that feudal structures—with their disregard for accountability and transparency and penchant for secrecy—no longer serve the church's mission. But our steps are unsure and we keep issuing edicts and proclamations and excommunications as if people are taking them seriously. Our long slumbering and repressed religious imagination broke into the light at the Second Vatican Council, but we simply couldn't tolerate its freedom and vitality. We came to fear that our certainties and absolute truths were at risk. We lost our nerve and allowed our creeds to trump our trust in Jesus Christ and the Holy Spirit. As *the* official teachers, many of our bishops believe they have nothing to learn from the laity, their priests, and vowed religious. Certainly, their certainties lead them to believe they have nothing to learn from our ecumenical and interfaith brothers and sisters. So they double the sentinels, crack down on our theologians, fire some of our most pastoral bishops, and censure the heart of our church—our faithful and prophetic sisters.

So I WALK THE STREETS OF MY virtual underground with my collar turned up and my cap pulled low—the secret police stand in the shadows—my eyes searching for a crack in the darkness, a flicker of light, a spark of hope. Whenever I can, I seek out friends and trail guides for coffee and serious conversation leading to blessed communion.

NOTES

[1] A. Schonmetzer and Heinrich Denzinger, eds., *Enchiridion symbolorum definitionum et declarationum de rebus fidei et morum,* 32nd ed. (Barcinone: Herder, 1963), 3903.

[2] Karl Rahner and Hilda C. Graef, *Grace in Freedom* (London: Burns & Oates, 1969), 117–18.

[3] Harvey Cox, *The Future of Faith* (New York: Harper-One, 2009), 6–7.

[4] Ibid., 106.

[5] James Carroll, *Practicing Catholic* (Boston: Houghton Mifflin Harcourt, 2010), 83.

[6] Jean Sulivan, *Morning Light: The Spiritual Journal of Jean Sulivan* (New York: Paulist Press, 1988), 122.

[7] Albert Nolan, *Jesus Today: A Spirituality of Radical Freedom* (Maryknoll, NY: Orbis Books, 2006), 132.

[8] Quoted in Cullen Murphy's *God's Jury: The Inquisition and the Making of the Modern World* (Boston: Houghton Mifflin Harcourt, 2012), 180.

[9] *America,* August 4–11, 2003, 11.

[10] *New York Times*, December 18, 2011.

[11] Alan Ehrenhalt, *The Lost City* (New York: Basic Books, 1995), 2.

[12] John L. McKenzie, *Authority in the Church* (New York: Sheed and Ward, 1966), 84.

[13] Isaiah 61:1–2.

[14] Charles Taylor, *A Secular Age* (Cambridge, MA: Belknap Press of Harvard University Press, 2007), 18.

[15] Ibid., 3.

[16] Ibid., 772.

[17] Thomas Merton, *Conjectures of a Guilty Bystander* (Garden City, NY: Doubleday, 1966), 142–48.

[18] Cited in Cox, *The Future of Faith,* 3.

[19] Thomas Merton, *Seeds of Contemplation* (Norfolk, CT: New Directions, 1949), 22.

[20] *Learning to Love: The Journals of Thomas Merton,* vol. 6, 1966–67, ed. Christine M. Bochen (New York: Harper Collins, 1997).

[21] Sulivan, *Morning Light,* 7.

[22] Leo Tolstoy, *War and Peace,* trans. Andrew Bromfield (New York: HarperCollins, 2000), 719.

[23] Paul Tillich and F. Forrester Church, *The Essential Tillich: An Anthology of the Writings of Paul Tillich* (New York: Macmillan, 1987), 102.